BRILLIANT AWAKENING:

20 STORIES OF HOPE & HEALING FROM THE MOUTHS OF EVERYDAY SHEROS

Paula McDade
Presenting the Amazing Co-Authors

Stellar Creative, LLC | Oklahoma City, OK

Printed in the United States of America

First Printing, 2017 | Createspace.com

ISBN 978-1545101223

Stellar Creative, LLC
11560 N. May Ave, #303
Oklahoma City, OK 73120

www.StellarCreates.com

Dedication

For those without a voice. Borrow our courage until you can find your own.

Co-Author Story Order

Paula McDade

Paula McDade is the Owner of Stellar Creative, LLC and the Creative Director behind The Brilliant Awakening, an anthology of stories from 20 women sharing their experiences and hope in overcoming trauma and abuse. She is the Founder and Visionary of the Not on My Watch Women's Initiative, a fiscally sponsored project of Social Good Fund. The mission of NOMWWI is to provide a gateway of advocacy, awareness, support and resources for women and girls affected by domestic violence, sexual abuse & assault, and mental illness. A sought after national Speaker, Author, and Creative Social Entrepreneur, Paula McDade inspires women to shake off the limits of the past, while breaking through the walls of doubt and fear by sharing her personal testimony.

Introduction

It is an amazing thing to watch human beings wake up to their purpose, their potential, and their power. This project has truly been a labor of love from the very beginning. Within 24 hours after announcing this book I already had a group of twelve women ready to dive in and get started. Several others quickly followed and the fearless twenty started to take shape. The extraordinary stories that follow is the result of countless hours of digging. These women dug deep into their heart and souls to pour out their very personal and transparent narratives. The work was hard and dirty, but they rose to the challenge. When they wanted to quit, I would not let them. I pushed, coached, and pep-talked until they felt sure they could press on. I often let them borrow my courage until they could muster their own. We talked of purpose, power, and a higher calling. Many of them simply wanted to get their stories out on paper to validate their own journey. If that is the only purpose for which this book was written, I will be satisfied that the work has been done.

You will laugh, cry, shout and rejoice as you read the stories of triumph over tragedy. There are no good guys and bad guys here. Every experience is a life lesson that has catapulted these brave souls into a new dimension of freedom and self-discovery. Like all of them, I have endured my own journey through hardship, trials, and trauma. I could identify with each of them in a very real and personal way. Even as I began work on this book, my own personal story was unfolding. I have often asked myself if I was up for the challenge of leading these women through what would be a life changing adventure while trying to navigate my own personal drama. The answer was a resounding yes! I knew I could not abandon the call that God had placed in my heart and I also knew that this was bigger than me. I said yes to more than a project, it was truly my destiny. I felt like a conductor leading those who were lost into their ultimate destination. I could not be more honored to serve these women and form lifelong bonds that will last far beyond the initial excitement of releasing this book.

Many will read these stories and wonder why. They will ask why someone would put so much of their personal and private business into a book for others to read. Others will understand and applaud the efforts of these brave sheros. I call them "Everyday Sheros" for a reason. In our daily lives, we have no idea who we are sitting next to on the church pew, who we are working with in the next cubicle. We assume things about people that may or may not be true based upon our own perception. It is not until you begin to hear their story that you understand the woman behind the daily roles they play. Their own personal struggles have created the landscape for the lives they now lead. Behind closed doors we cannot begin to know the tears they have cried and the wounds they have nurtured in private. Emotional pain is a pain like no other. When you break a bone, or endure an injury there are remedies you can apply to immediately ease the pain. A cast or split, a bandage or ointment can bring immediate relief. When there is emotional trauma the cure often takes lots of time, attention, and prayer.

As you read these stories, I hope you will see yourself in the pages or perhaps someone you know. Keep your heart and mind open for the light at the end of each page. Some of us are still in the process while others have overcome and moved on to other challenges. One thing is for sure, this book could be filled with the stories of people you know personally or complete strangers. The impact is the same. Stories empower and heal. I am glad you decided to pick up a copy for yourself or someone you know. I thank you for thinking enough to invest in the personal empowerment of the women on these pages. We are humbled and grateful to have the opportunity to share something very special with you.

Love & Light,
Paula McDade | Creative Director, The Brilliant Awakening

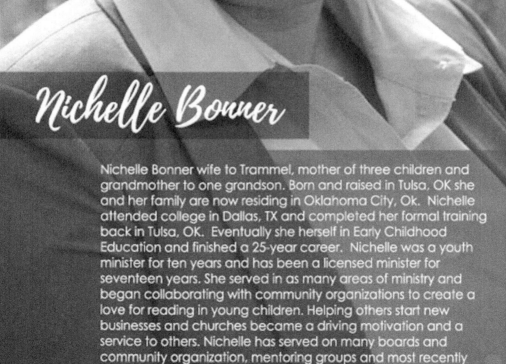

Nichelle Bonner

Nichelle Bonner wife to Trammel, mother of three children and grandmother to one grandson. Born and raised in Tulsa, OK she and her family are now residing in Oklahoma City, Ok. Nichelle attended college in Dallas, TX and completed her formal training back in Tulsa, OK. Eventually she herself in Early Childhood Education and finished a 25-year career. Nichelle was a youth minister for ten years and has been a licensed minister for seventeen years. She served in as many areas of ministry and began collaborating with community organizations to create a love for reading in young children. Helping others start new businesses and churches became a driving motivation and a service to others. Nichelle has served on many boards and community organization, mentoring groups and most recently serves on the Advisory Board of the Not on My Watch Women's Initiative.

"Lesson Learned"

Growing up in the mid-west as a church girl with lots of friends and a huge family I was very naive about life. My biggest dream was to become a pianist. I loved watching, hearing, and playing the piano. That soon faded when I stepped into high school. A few of my friends and I started a dance group and we were popular in our school but more importantly we had fun dancing. Our school had a yearly talent show and we decided we would audition for it. We wanted to see if we could compete with the older kids and make it on this talent show called "Hi-Jinks". We made the cut and how excited we were to participate! I was so happy during this time having fun with my friends. Life was good and school was great.

Friday evening was the biggest night of the show and a friend and I are standing outside watching the door. I noticed a guy looking at me but he wasn't saying anything. He just stared he would look away and then stare some more. The very next week at school, a girl came up to me. She handed me a paper with a name and number on it. She said this guy wants to meet you and wants you to call him. I told her no, because I was already dating another guy that I really liked, but as most teenage relationships go it did not last long. When the relationship failed, my feelings were a little hurt but I decided to move on.

I called this guy and he was surprised to hear from me because of the amount of time that had gone by. I ended up connecting with him and life as I knew it was about to change. He was six years older than I was, didn't have a steady job and he lived with his family. His upbringing was different than mine. He had a lot of life experience that I did not have. I only wish that the alarms would have gone off in my head and warned me not to get involved at all but that did not happen for me. I began a life experience that I would never ever forget.

He said simple things that got my attention. He showed an interested in me, my color, my shape, my height. He noticed small things about me and complimented me on those things. Those trivial things were a big deal to me. It wasn't always cool to have full lips, a curvy shape or to be a dark-skinned girl. He took the time to notice me and he always made me feel good about how I looked. He was picking me up for lunch from school and sometimes he would bring me lunch. Other times he would take my friends and me to lunch. He took me to concerts, and we spent all my free time together or on the phone. As time progressed now I would only see my friends at school. I began hanging around with him and his friend. I would go where he took me. He started buying me clothes and things that any 15-year-old girl would enjoy. This is where things began to go wrong. Other girls my age started to come around and they would argue and fight right in front of me. These were warning signs that something was wrong, but I was the good girl, naive and not street smart. That was one of the things he said he liked about me which I later found out why.

As time went on I made an adult decision on immature emotions. I decided that he would be the one that I would go all the way with. In my mind, he was showing me all the attention, love and affection I thought that I needed and wanted. I decided that one day soon I would not be the good girl anymore. I thought that would make our relationship last because he would be my first. What I didn't know is that I would be opening myself up to a different world than what I imagined. What began in my mind as teenage love with an older guy turned into a nightmare that I didn't know how to escape. The fights between him and other girls progressed. They would shout things at me about him and say that he was lying to me. They would say they were pregnant by him or they just had a child by him. Then my senior year in high school I got pregnant! This was not part of the plan. My parents would be so disappointed. I knew it would send my mother through the roof! She was adamant that I was to have nothing to do with this older guy but as you can see I didn't listen. I was afraid and didn't want to tell my parents what I had done. Alone was the worst feeling in the world for this teenaged pregnant girl.

His first response was denial (surprise) and he didn't call or see me for weeks until I decided to do the unthinkable. I decided to just get rid of the baby. I was clueless about the procedure and too scared to ask for help. He forked over the money for me to go through with it and I didn't hear anything else from him for two months. Then out of nowhere I get a call from him with an apology. I wish I had run away but remember I just aborted my first child with no one to talk to and no one had any idea of what I was going through. Connecting with who I thought was a friend was welcomed. The long nights of crying and not understanding what happened and what I had done was not going away easily. I began thinking I just wanted to be normal and happy again.

I graduated and I left for business school six months later. At that time, he was still a big part of my life. I had heard many lies and he has become very accusing, manipulating and distant from me. When we would talk on the phone, he'd say "you were out meeting guys". He always wanted to know who I talked to on the phone and at school. He accused my roommates of bringing friends to meet me. He would say that he knew what I was doing. He'd also say he had people watching me all the time. There would be surprise visits trying to catch me talking to other guys. It never stopped and I was always concerned about his feelings. I did not notice that I was doing exactly what he wanted me to do. I was staying to myself and not talking to people or making new friends at school. Meanwhile, he was doing whatever he wanted with whomever he wanted. If I questioned him he would accuse my friends and family of trying to break us up, lying on him or trying to get with him. I would feel obligated to make sure he knew that I wanted and was faithful to him. Each day I felt more like I was in a cage with no freedom to live my life.

My parents had no idea what was going on. The entire time I was at school, this guy chose to continue playing with my emotions, and feelings. I did not have the energy to argue over the constant lies, deceptions, and insecurities. He continued to accuse me of seeing other people and looking up ex boyfriends. Girls kept coming around while I was trying to recover from an abortion and attend school. He was still getting girls pregnant. I still didn't know that I was seeing signs trying to tell me to pay attention. I was being groomed and had no idea that this older guy had picked a young naive girl that could be trained easily.

The very next year I thought things were good. My friends and I decided to go to the doctor to get birth control. At the end of the visit they called all my friends and they were finished. I was called into the office to be told I needed to call my parents and start prenatal care. You should have seen the look on my face after hearing those words again. I thought God was punishing me because of the abortion I had the previous year. Even though the fear came up again a small part of me was happy to know that God didn't punish me. Now I had to decide how to be brave enough to tell my parents, but this time I would have to do it. Another abortion was not in my plan; the first one was hard enough. I had to call the same guy again after remembering how the first time did not go so well. As my friends and I left the clinic still in disbelief, this group of girls was so encouraging and supportive. Some of them I had just met a few months prior and they helped me mentally and emotionally during that time in my life. I am still so grateful to those young women.

I made the calls with the help of God, first to my parents to give them the news. Whatever I said and however I said it must have been okay for them. My parents sent my male friend to pack up all my belonging and bring me home. Can you imagine my face to see him there on my door step instead of my parents? As time went on, I now had two children and then the physical abuse began. Now, instead of questioning me, I was being pushed, shoved, and slapped around. One day I decided to ask him who he was talking to on the pay phone in front of a store. He dragged me around to the back of the building and began to beat me. When he was finished with me he told me to get up and that it was all my fault that it happened. The whole time I'm driving home and as we get onto the highway, he was fussing and punching me in the face. When we got to our destination I just wanted to go home but now he wouldn't let me leave until I forgave him. I heard the promises that it would not happen again and so on. Just so I could go home I agreed.

One day I was preparing to leave the house. He wanted to know how I was getting to work, but my answer wasn't good enough so he began to chase me around the apartment. I had been ironing my clothes so I picked up the iron and raised it at him and screamed for him to leave. He left so I took off with my children and the clothes on my back never to return. That was the end of that chapter of my life.

The best part about this journey is my beautiful boys from this. The best part is that God brought me out of that mental and physical abuse I endured. Then God gave me the opportunity to reach back and help other women young and old come out also. This was not the end of my story but the beginning of a new chapter. For that God I am thankful and grateful to you!

Premadonna Braddick

Premadonna Braddick is an Actress, Ordained minster, Life coach, Author, and a prime example of overcoming less than desirable circumstances. She was born and raised in the foster care system in Oakland, California from age two to eighteen. She spent the early years of her life dealing with depression, low self-esteem, and a poor self-image. Despite this, she was surrounded by mentors who offered guidance, wisdom, and inspired her to pursue her purpose in life, and therefore understands the importance of mentor-ship. Instead of using her past as an excuse, Premadonna turned her obstacles into stepping stones to achieve her own goals, and help other young women and teenage girls do the same.

"Re-Write Your Story"

"Please Mom; I will do it better next time. I didn't mean to do it that way I am really trying." "No, you're not you're just trying to be defiant towards me, and I am going to teach you what happens to defiant kids like you who willingly disobeys me."

Charmaine's face was fear stricken as she was terrified to know what her foster mother was going to do to her next. Her foster mother yanked her from the chair by her arm, but Charmaine was mercifully pleading with her, "Please Mom, I'm sorry; I won't do it again, I promise I will try harder."

It seemed the more Charmaine pleaded her foster mother; she seemed to have more and more of a deaf ear. Charmaine looked at her foster father screaming, "Please Daddy, save me." He too looked helplessly back at Charmaine as her foster mother was dragging her from the table. Charmaine looked over at her foster sister in the hope she would be her saving grace to say something to her mother to stop doing this to her sister, but instead, she put her head down as if she didn't see or hear or see anything that was going on.

Charmaine's heart was racing as she struggled to get away from the tight grip of her foster mother's hand on her arm while she was dragging her down the hall. Charmaine continued to kick and scream for her foster daddy to help her. "Daddy, please help me; don't let her do this to me please!!" Charmaine was dragged to the bathroom her foster mother turned on the water then turned and started beating Charmaine in the face and head.

"Shut up, you stupid girl, I am going to teach you a lesson; this will be the last time you defy me." Then it happened; she forced Charmaine's head in the running water. Charmaine was struggling for air and to get free, but her foster mother strength was too strong for Charmaine's fragile 10-year-old-body to fight her anymore, she eventually passed out.

She doesn't know how long she was out, but she was awakened by the voice of her foster mother who said to her daughter standing over Charmaine, "This is how you treat defiant and stupid kids, I bet she won't do that again." So, what was the wrongdoing that Charmaine did that caused her to be harshly disciplined? Sadly, it was because she didn't properly hold her knife and fork, right? Yes, her foster mother was angry because Charmaine was having difficulty cutting her meat, and for that, she was beaten.

This young girl, Charmaine, was actually me. This memory of me at 10 years old still troubles me today, but not in a way where I allow this painful memory to dictate my life. But, instead, it's a reminder of how God took my pain for His gain to be a voice to countless of other children and teenagers who were victims of emotional and physical abuse. For many years, I suffered from depression, insecurities, low self-esteem, anxieties, and suicidal ideations.

My story started with two drug addict parents who lived their lives in and out of jail. When my mother gave birth to me, she was in jail; she couldn't take me home because she had to finish her sentence in jail. So, the next place I should have been sent home to was my maternal grandmother, but that couldn't happen because my mother and grandmother were both serving time at the Alameda County Jail. My mother was eventually released but continued to live a transient life that was not safe for baby. She was so fixated on her drug lifestyle that my dad said she left me at Jack-In- the Box, and it was there I was put into state custody at age two, and I remained there until I was 18 years old. My social worker said the severe trauma I endured as a young child caused me to have a speech impediment, to be emotionally disturbed, and to be delayed. More than likely, I would have an unsuccessful life.

My story taught me to wear a mask and smile through my emotional pain. Heck, I smiled so much that I was voted best smile twice in junior high. But, no matter how much I smiled and pretended these crippling thoughts didn't exist, I found myself drowning further in a dark hole. The mask I wore was a way to avoid my past. However, when one avoids their painful past, it cannot only affect your present life, but it can also disrupt your future. The only way to heal from the past is to deal and face what you have been running away from. You can accomplish this by asking God to heal every area in your life.

The questions I had for God were, "How do I heal from this? What meaning do I have in my life?" I was determined to get my healing, and I wasn't going to give up. Because of my persistence, I was able to find why I suffered from depression for so many years. That answer came from my graduate program at ORU where I received two masters in the field of counseling. What I learned in my counseling classes is that I wasn't crazy, and my emotional symptoms were real and nothing I caused, but they steamed from the broken family system I came from that left me shattered. When I learned this fact, it was now up to me to take control of my life and no longer accept the narrative that was passed down to me.

So, how do I re-write a story from a bad hand dealt to me? I first had to find forgiveness for my bio parents and foster mother. When I speak of forgiveness, it doesn't mean forgetting but mainly giving yourself a gift to be free from emotional bondage. I learned that I could no longer be a caged bird sequestered in my feelings of unforgiveness, anger, and resentment, but instead open the cage doors and soar like an eagle with no distress. Once that was accomplished, I found meaning in my life and held on to the words from a concentration camp survivor Victor Frankl who said: "That it is the sense of meaning that enables people to overcome painful experience in their lives." My painful childhood experience was not the end of my story but instead the beginning. Through the years, I found there were many chapters in my life that had meaning and lessons that helped me to be wiser and mentally stronger. My meaning gave me hope that if I can overcome something so traumatic than I can encourage other ladies and teen girls to do the same too.

In my chapters of my life, I learned that you cannot allow person's negative opinion or even a statistic define your future. Studies show that 70% of foster care children who aged out of foster care within two years will be incarcerated. Yes, incarceration was the story of my family. I have to honestly say I too have been in a prison system, just as my family, but this time I was there as a motivational speaker to other women who were incarcerated. I gave them hope that just because they're incarcerated doesn't mean their children will follow after them. The devil's predicted future is that your life is going to be what the society thinks you may turn out and we somehow join in alliance with that story and sadly create an environment that stifles us to move forward and beyond our circumstances. But my dear Daughter and Sister, God has a preferred future for you where you are shining; you're growing, and most of all living and not just existing.

That little scared Charmaine who felt rejected, unloved, and thought she had no identity later found out that Charmaine was my middle name and Premadonna was actually my first name, but the social workers refused to call me by my first name. For many years, I felt insignificant but soon learned that Premadonna in Italian means first lady. So, I carried a name and a purpose in me that was hidden because I accepted the name that was said to me. How many times have we done that to ourselves? We carry a great purpose and gift inside of us, but because we hear the labels, others say we conceal who God call us to be.

Know that everyone in your life may not be in your next chapter. Maybe that's where the road ends for them. God met you where you were. You had to be wounded to know He's a healer. You had to come from a place where trust was exempt to know that you can trust God for Him to be the author of your story so you can live a successful, self-sufficient, and holistic life!!

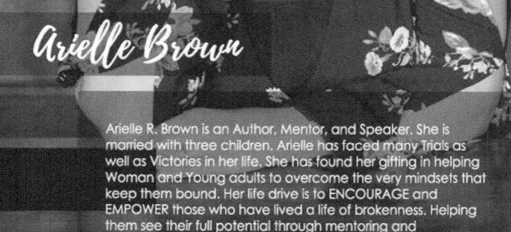

Arielle Brown

Arielle R. Brown is an Author, Mentor, and Speaker. She is married with three children. Arielle has faced many Trials as well as Victories in her life. She has found her gifting in helping Woman and Young adults to overcome the very mindsets that keep them bound. Her life drive is to ENCOURAGE and EMPOWER those who have lived a life of brokenness. Helping them see their full potential through mentoring and relationship building. From this passion, she birthed her blog "Raising Royalty".

"Undressed"

As a young girl, I just wanted to be noticed and loved with unconditional love. One that I knew would fulfill my longing for a father. I looked up to every man that was in my life. I searched all over for a father figure that I could find my protection in. I wanted someone that would wipe my tears when I cried and one that would be so proud of all my accomplishments that I achieved.

Instead, when I was six years old, my world turned upside down by a man I looked up to. I will never forget the day my mother went out for the night and dropped me off at my grandparents. She thought the place was the safest she had for me to be. After all, she just wanted to let her hair down and enjoy the night.

That night, my grandmother got me ready for bed. She then told me to go lay down on her side of the bed. In this bed was my grandfather wrestling to go to sleep. I rolled over and said goodnight. I remember him saying goodnight and saying to come closer as he would comfort me from the storm that night. I remember being a bit uncomfortable as he wrapped his arms around me. I tried to push back the memories of previous days. After all, it must be partly my fault, right? Just as I began to close my eyes that night, I started feeling the hands that were ever so familiar run across my fragile little body. Starting on my stomach and slowly and gently making its way into my pajama pants. I began to cringe and shake. I was so scared I didn't know what I did so wrong or even how this could be right. In my mind, I was screaming: *PLEASE STOP TOUCHING ME!* All the while my lips stayed closed, and I began to feel the most confusing feeling in the world. A sensation that should have never been felt until the day I was married to the love of my life. Instead, that sensation of my clitoris being fondled was now associated with a horrific experience.

Every time the thunder would boom I would jump, and it wasn't because of the thunder. It was because I was so scared and I was just praying he would see that and stop. Instead, he just reassured me everything was just fine and that I had no need to be scared he had me. As he kept touching me and satisfying himself, I began to associate the deep breath that blew on my back as disgusting and painful.

After he was done, he told me goodnight and kept me close. At that moment, all I could think was, *Please, Mommy, come get me.* All I want is her to embrace me and tell me I was going to be okay. Contrary to what I wanted, I laid there and fell asleep looking forward to the morning to come.

I woke up early that next morning to find my grandmother making food in the kitchen and my grandfather still asleep. At that moment, my heart began to race as I went to tell my grandmother everything that happened the night before. It was a thought that would not ever leave my mind. So, I built up courage and asked my grandma if I could tell her a secret. She reassured me it would be kept between us. I proceeded to tell her that Grandpa kept touching me in my panties and that I wanted her to tell my mother. She did not seem to be bothered as much as I was by it. She never made me feel gross or wrong. Then again, she did not even act like it was abnormal. She replied, "I will tell her. You do not need to tell her. Let me tell her."

At this moment, I just said, "Okay" and walked away. I felt violated and disconnected.

When my mom finally pulled up to get me, I ran and hugged her and did not want her to leave my side. I was waiting for my grandmother to pull her to the side and tell her my secret. Instead, she gave me a deep look as to say I better not say anything.

We then all said our goodbyes. My mother then took me to the car and buckled me up. She began asking how my time with my grandparents was. I proceeded to say, "Mommy, I do not want you to be mad at me, but I have to tell you this. Grandpa keeps touching me, and I do not like it." In mid-sentence, I began to cry. Her eyes filled up with tears.

She then stopped the car and replied, "Why would I be mad at you? It's going to be okay Arielle; I love you."

At that moment, my mother rushed me to the hospital to have a rape kit done on me. Everything from that point on began to happen so fast. Multiple doctors and hospital staff came rushing into the room. My mother is standing by my head kissing my forehead and letting me know it was going to all be okay. All the while I am lying there with my legs wide open to a room full of people I don't even know. My heart began to sink to my stomach, and they handed me a towel to lay over my eyes as the proceeded with the rape kit.

When this was all said and done, I, a six-year-old girl, was left with one of the biggest scars of my entire life etched so deep in my soul. This scar would direct the path for many years to come. This was a scar that thrust me into a world of walls that I have built on the inside. In this world, sex and intimacy no longer had the same definition. They did not even go together. Sex was just an act that I did to find the only attention I knew I would get.

Something was deposited into my soul that night that attracted what seemed to be a world full of evil. As grew older, I found myself not knowing my worth or who I was. I had been used, abused, and rejected. I walked into many situations looking for love but with a deficit that had yet to be filled. One that needed healing before I even needed to seek outside of myself for what was missing.

I needed to unlearn my reality as truth and relearn the love that I had never felt before. After molestation, physical abuse, rejection, and so much more. I found myself in a place seeking something greater to heal what I could not heal on my very own. In that low place where I was, high on ecstasy, I began to cry out to the only God I knew of. The one I heard about in the times I went to church as a child, yet, the one I never really encountered for myself; this God I only heard people previously give testimonies about. I found myself looking into the mirror of the dressing room at the strip club I was then working in as a dancer, saying to myself, "I am worth so much more. This cannot be all there is to life." After that moment, God began to pursue me like never before.

When I realized I was broken and in need of a Savior, He did what only He could do best. He began to show me an intimacy that I found myself trying to reject. He came into a place where I tried so hard to build a wall around in my life. He began using men in the strip club to speak life to me and tell me that I am not a woman for that place. They could see me in Los Angeles, working in executive offices and so much more. I knew then that God was calling me out of my valley and lifting me to a place of healing.

This was the start of my Journey with Christ. I fell many times in this six-year-journey. I even found myself looking back to my old bondage in low moments of my now free life. I would never have imagined I would be writing my story to you this day. I just want to encourage you to fight the good fight; there is a way out. The process is beautiful. The beauty of the process though is when God completes His work it never has to be touched up again. You can be free. Shift your perspective to Christ and shift from healing to wholeness.

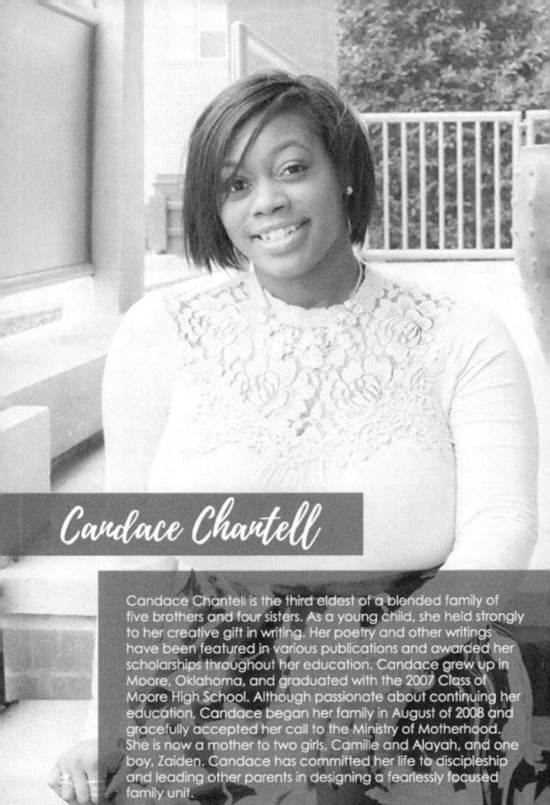

Candace Chantell

Candace Chantell is the third eldest of a blended family of five brothers and four sisters. As a young child, she held strongly to her creative gift in writing. Her poetry and other writings have been featured in various publications and awarded her scholarships throughout her education. Candace grew up in Moore, Oklahoma, and graduated with the 2007 Class of Moore High School. Although passionate about continuing her education, Candace began her family in August of 2008 and gracefully accepted her call to the Ministry of Motherhood. She is now a mother to two girls, Camille and Alayah, and one boy, Zaiden. Candace has committed her life to discipleship and leading other parents in designing a fearlessly focused family unit.

"Mind Games"

The only reason to look back is to remember why you must keeping going forward. The reason I couldn't escape the prison of my mind was because I refused to realize that I deserved better. *No one deserves anything*, were the words I replayed as I would try and tell myself this is not the life for me. I didn't deserve such entitlement. But, am I not entitled to be loved? When you take in its context the definition: to be worthy of, it is hard to place yourself at the beginning of that statement. *I, Candace Chantel, I am worthy of love.*

Like most, I felt my story to be insignificant. I discarded many memories because I knew there were far too many women that had endured worse than I. You see I had not been touched inappropriately by a loving family member, nor was I forced to endure lustful acts. However, I still have a story to share. It is past time that my voice is heard.

I had dreamed of marriage. Like most girls, I played house with my dolls and friends. We all looked forward to the day someone would get down on one knee and ask us to spend the rest of our life with him. My day had finally come, and although he was late to arrive, I rejected the warning signs as I reassured myself he was certain God told him I was the one. Now, my faith was dependent on those around me. It was what God had done for my family and friends that made me feel like I knew Him personally. I didn't know that God would talk to me too.

Like most of my relationships, I gave him all of me too soon. I wasn't the type to get clingy at first sight and ramble sweet I love you's from the beginning. However, sex was my specialty, and I felt it to be my due diligence to let him and anyone else before him in pursuit know just what I was bringing to the table. I was unaware that I was more than an object of satisfaction. I say pursuit but to be quite honest, now that I have matured, I can confess I have never been pursued nor have I truly dated anyone with proper intentions aligned with proper boundaries and standards. Growing up, I remember one of my family members telling me that all any guy would want from me is sex; therefore, I made sure sex was what I had on display.

As our marriage progressed, his true self began to unfold, or possibly it already had, and I chose to ignore it. He would time me coming home from work. If I didn't have a healthy cooked meal prepared, then I was assumed to be a bad wife. There were no days off; the house needed dusting and laundry needed to be washed, dried, and folded into its proper drawer. No became an all too familiar response to invites outside of the home. He would complain that I didn't make enough money; so, in an effort to do my part, I would quit jobs with no hesitation to attain more money. My resume is proof that I am skilled in various areas of expertise, but I developed a terrible work ethic of not staying in any place longer than a year. My wardrobe was bland and no matter how sexy and confident I thought I was, for him, it simply wasn't good enough.

I remember the feeling of defeat. It was like having my eyes open but only seeing black, unable to take a step because any direction would lead me down a rocky slope that never reached its end. His words would replay in my head without pause making it even harder to breathe in-between the toxic waste that hoarded my mental space. *If I can't be enough for him, I will never be enough for anyone.* Even after the divorce, there were entirely too many self-improvements needed for any man to consider looking my way. He had defined me. I'm not sure whether to place blame on my lack of experience or my young age. Others were okay with just having babies and no strings attached, but I wanted the happily-ever-after. I believed love could be and would be just that.

I remember my car breaking down in Norman, and, even though months had passed between us, I knew he would come. So, despite my core reminding me of the minimal growth I had made, I fell deep into the quicksand of his apologies and we began again, only this time things had gotten worse. Ladies, if I could for a minute advise you that a man of God should plant seed everywhere he walks. Simply attending church and quoting scriptures is not enough. Even the Pharisees knew the Law of Moses yet followed their own will *(Matthew 23).* Similarly, this dog talked like a dog but slithered like a snake.

One Mother's Day I was accused of incest because my daughter looked too much like my cousin. It was as if he would purposely hold onto his bitterness for times I was with my family, knowing all too well the chains he had drilled into my mind would nag at me the rest of the day. We were evicted for some unknown reason, simply because I allowed him to handle everything. He found shelter for himself and left me alone to find a dwelling for my daughter and myself, despite his residence having spare rooms to accommodate us all. I walked several miles downtown waiting for him to pick me up from work. After that, I gained just enough dignity to call for a taxi. I was chased around the house during arguments fearful that I would be beaten for finally using my voice. He made jokes about his gun that he purposely kept in our bedroom, knowing all too well I did not agree with firearms inside the house. He was my very own devil.

I stared at the pill bottles in the cabinet, calculating how many of each would be necessary to end the torment of the mind games. I had been fighting for far too long, and at that time I failed to realize that every day I lived was another day I had won. As I stared at the suicide letter I had just written I felt a deeper part of me cry out for victory. There was a part of me that had been buried yet still desired to live.

Over time, God had been using a dear friend to speak confidence into me. Every time I left her house I gave him a sure piece of my mind. Bre was my saving grace during one of the roughest storms of my life. It was her faithfulness as a single mother that I found the most comfort. One day, she told me my words to him meant nothing until my actions followed them. With that, I went the next day and applied for an apartment, I came home and told him he had until the end of the month to move his things out. He was gone that weekend. I was free. After him leaving nothing went as planned.

We had racked up over $1000 in OGE bills, in my name, which left my daughter and me in the dark for several days. Furniture was also financed in my name; these negative loans had affected my rental process. Without my consent, he called our landlord and gave him the okay to lease our duplex, and just like that my daughter and I were homeless again. The only thing different about this time was that my worship never wavered. I was so full of joy. I trusted God completely. I was down to three days in the house, and it was at my sister-in-law's birthday. There I met a phenomenal widow who had extended her home to my daughter and me. She was a complete stranger. I didn't have to pray on it because I had already been praying, and I knew with all my being that everything would be okay.

I would love to say that my life has since been full of more highs than lows. I was struggling with every antagonistic comment that had ever been thrown at me as if my brain had been tracking negative logs. My mental imprisonment went far deeper than I was ready to accept. Creatively, the beauty behind the buried ashes of this story is that the very same God that delivered me will stop at nothing to see me wearing the crown of life for remaining steadfast during my trials. *(James1:12)* It is with this that I have discovered my identity in Him. I am fearlessly focused and fulfilled.

Karla Chapman

Karla Chapman is a wife, a busy mother of four beautiful sons, and a proud Christian woman. After graduating high school, Karla immediately enrolled into the U.S. Air Force. During her time in the military, she has been offered several opportunities to flourish in mentorship and leadership. She was hand-selected to teach Suicide Awareness training, focusing on warning signs and prevention. In 2013, Karla became an Air Force Master Resiliency Trainer. In addition to being a proud member of the Armed Forces, she is a life coach through her own business interests with Herbalife Nutrition. She is also the Founder and Creator of Radiate Your Resilience, a blog created to inspire individuals to live their best life, especially in the face of adversity.

When the Past Knocks, Open It: Radiating through the Shame

"Every adversity, every failure, every heartache carries with it the seed of an equal or greater benefit."
- Napoleon Hill

I believe when you are amid an awakening, you experience things from your past that make you see things differently than you ever had before. What had once been a cloud of myths or beliefs may now be as clear as glass to you. Awakenings are often the heart-wrenching realities of your true self. A glimpse who you really are; you may see yourself as a failure, wondering why you are in the place that you are at this moment. What once was forgotten or pushed under a rug may have been re-sparked by another event that happened in your past.

Two years ago, my whole world turned around. I wasn't sure if I would survive during this time and many people didn't know about it. What was happening to me, I now understand, was part of my continuous journey of awakening. Let me take you through the beginning of what I call, "Girl, wake up!"

In January of 2015, I separated from my husband. I did this with zero notice to anyone. It wasn't broadcasted, what was going on within the doors of my old-school, tiny household. What everyone saw was the "picture perfect" family, bright-eyed kids, and a husband and wife who adored one another, full of life and smiles. Every picture expressed pure love and promise. What I couldn't show is the heart-ache of what I truly felt on the inside. Only two months before that, I found out that not only was I with someone who kept secrets from me, but he was an alcoholic and gambler. In faith, I stayed with him even though he continued to live this lifestyle. The thing is, I didn't only concentrate on what was happening, but I immediately blamed myself. I was a perfectionist and wondered w*hat did KARLA do? Why hadn't I seen this? I see everything!* I know you may be wondering, as I have, why I didn't see this coming. It's a normal reaction and one I am guilty of, wondering why a spouse doesn't foresee events happening within their relationship.

When I separated from my husband, I was at my lowest. Misusing my own skills as a coach, I trained myself to believe that what was happening was "good." I trained this militant mind to cope with whatever came my way, refusing to deal with the situation at hand. The truth is I was doing it all wrong. My truth was I was mad as hell! I wondered if I even deserved the life that I had.

The life that I experienced with this man during those two years was a life of uncertainty and distrust. I didn't sleep anymore, and on numerous occasions, I stayed awake for 24 hours, afraid to sleep because I feared for my husband's life. I became a walking zombie, running on pure fumes to survive.

During these times of distress, I felt alone, as if no one understood me. I also felt as if I gave in, and expressed how I really felt, I would disappoint so many others that I had encouraged. What I didn't know was God was using me constantly in this process, allowing me to face my beginnings.

When I was just a small, six-year-old; vibrant and curious about the world, a big fingerprint was added to the chapters within my self-book. I was molested. Unfortunately, I am not the only one who has experienced this, and it saddens me. I am only a mere glimpse of what the act of abuse can do. After years of enduring this, hiding it from others, and getting little help due to the feeling of embarrassment and shame, I went through continuous battles within myself. I was marked.

What is this mark you ask? It is the mark that many of us have. We are abused, molested, mistreated, and forgotten about. We are often mishandled in our fragile states and more times than we can count on our hands, we experience depression, PTSD, and other mental health illnesses that are ignored in our households and communities.

When you go through things in your youth, it's clear that it may just happen to affect the things you experience through adolescence and adulthood. My youth was circled around being the best that I can be. I was always hiding how I really felt with a smile and when puberty hit... wow. I thought I was in love with every boy who gave me some sort of attention. In my adulthood, I experienced the same things, times 12. I cried more, argued more, protected myself more, and felt like I wasn't worthy... even MORE.

I recall on a weekday morning, my neighbor below me, a small, frail woman, knocking on my door. I ignored the knock for a while, nervous to even answer. After whispering to the kids, "don't make a sound," I looked through the peephole and asked, "Who is it?" She told me who she was and said that one of my belongings had fallen from my balcony to hers. When she raised her hand up, I knew it was mine, a pair of glasses that we had been looking for feverishly. I went on to tell her it wasn't mine, in fear of opening the door. After that incident, I knew something just wasn't right. This wasn't the first time that I had experienced fright over simple things, over-evaluating my surroundings in fear of pain caused to myself and my children.

In the summer of 2016, I was diagnosed with PTSD. It was one the most embarrassing moments of my life. Me, the woman who "has it all together" was diagnosed with a mental illness? Me, the woman who is a trained Resiliency Coach, not able to get her mind right. I was disgusted with myself and my life. I was isolating myself, and because of this, my children suffered. We stayed home from events if there were too many people out. I stopped answering phone calls, and I stayed in bed as much as I could. I wondered why I wasn't loved by God many times during this process. I know what I wanted and what I wanted to be like for my family, and I was not even close, to say the least. I was a hot mess! On the outside, I continued to hide what I was going through, but on the inside, the war was at its peak. I was having random outbursts, throwing things, and blaming others for where I was currently located on the map. I had traveled to the depths of hell and back, or what I thought. I never once during these moments took the time to realize the reason why I was in such pain, allowing myself to be in numerous relationships that ended with hurt and abuse, also abusing my own self, due to lack of self-love.

God woke me up a long time ago. When I say long, I am sure I was awake the minute my eyes were introduced to this new world. Yes, it sounds crazy, but when God is working, He works! The nanosecond I was born, like everyone else, our stories began. Some of us experience the same types of things, but just as he created unique fingerprints, he created unique stories within our lives here on Earth. I have grown to understand the process of life. Due to the acts of my husband, I was reintroduced to my traumas full force. I lived in constant fear, afraid to relive those moments. From this process, God led me to face my past head on. I believe if this situation hadn't happened, I would have continued living a secret life.

God has ways of taking your pains, trials, and mistakes and turning them into something good. What some would consider a horrible act, I have found the new meaning of love. When you can love a person, even through the pain that they have caused you, you will know that God is inside you. What some may call a burden, I call a success story. I have embraced my PTSD, understanding that this disease is not only military-based but can happen to anyone. Every day I find a new way to live in the moment, loving the life that I am still able to enjoy. I don't concentrate on the past. Instead, I look to the future with hopes of healing and a healthy lifestyle for myself and family.

Whatever traumas you may be experiencing, know that you are not alone; God is with you. Call out to Him, and He will flip your story in such a way. He will give you His eyes for you to find peace and awaken your soul. He will protect and shield you and love you more than you can ever imagine. He will place other people within your life to help you grow and to tell you: You are unique, beautiful, and enough! Your life on this Earth is on purpose! Be you! Radiate!

Kara Cline

Kara Cline is a mother, sister, daughter and friend. She earned a degree in business and broadcast journalistm from Rose State College and OCCC. Since 2009, Kara has been a top performer in the promotional marketing and advertising industry, representing many major brands and broadcast media outlets. She is currently co-launching a mobile app called "Revenue Retriever". She has also received her certification in Behavioral Health Case Management. Kara mentors young girls in her community and volunteers at her local school. She puts God first and hopes to be a light to others.

"Release Your Resistance"

I began writing by making little notes. As I jotted stuff down, I had to take a step back and regroup. I went from, "Can I handle this?" to, "I can do this… BUT do I want everyone to know my story?"

The answer is YES! Hopefully, it encourages growth and healing. God's will lead me to survive my situation. So, in His honor, I would like to take this written opportunity to praise the Lord. He brought me out of a very abusive relationship and has blessed me with more favors than ever imagined. Through faith, God has and will help us in our darkest moments. There's nothing like prayer. I ask to you, please pray often. Know with prayer comes work. Prayer without works is dead. Life's too short to be unhappy. If you want to change, you must be the one to change.

It took me years to learn this. I thought if I am consistent others will change. If I'm a good kid, my Mom will love me. If I'm a good friend, I'll be popular. If I'm a good girlfriend, I'll fall in love, get married, have kids and live happily ever after. I HAD IT ALL FIGURED OUT! I thought if I kept it real, people would keep it real with me. Turns out, to most, keeping it real is just a saying. It's like swimming with sharks; you must learn to ride the wave.

Being naive to this, I got mixed up with the wrong guy early on. I picked the wrong person and coincidently sabotaged my high school days… Prom… Graduation parties… It was my Senior Trip… 4th of July. August came, I hadn't enrolled in college; although, I received many letters. Significant milestones quickly passed. Months turned into years of abuse.

As a child, I swore to never date an abusive guy. My family has had generations of abuse. My grandmother was abused by my grandfather. Their son, my father, abused my mother. My mom would've tripped out had she known. I was a good kid with a 4.0 GPA and a ton of potential. I had truly dumbed myself down to be with him.

Things I endured:

- My home had kicked in doors, broken tables, holes in the wall, and never a bed.
- My car became his ride. He broke windows, slashed tires, and never paid to fix anything.
- Going out with friends was unheard of; therefore, I spent many Friday nights sitting on the porch, drinking by myself.
- Fists were being thrown at my head daily; always pointless arguments.

- Dark eye shadow was my go-to for covering black eyes.
- Long-sleeved shirts became a necessity to hide bruised arms and bite marks.
- Constantly accused of cheating but actually being cheated on.

I REGRET not walking away the first time I was hit. I moved out from my Mom's house to be controlled by my supposed equal, my classmate, my boyfriend. He had manipulated me. No longer able to be myself, work was my only getaway. He let me have a job to keep money in his pockets. He didn't work. Everything became my responsibility.

Punches got harder, healing time longer. My gut told me to leave, but I was in denial. Instead, I made a million reasons to stay, and I did. You probably wonder what reason could be good enough. Today I honestly couldn't tell you. Back then my mind was crazy.

I asked myself:

- Where was I to go? If he found me, he would beat me up and bring me back.
- Who was I going to ask for help? I was too embarrassed to tell my mom. Plus, I didn't want to let her down.
- How do I start over? I thought I was in love. I felt like he needed me, or I needed him. As a true friend, I wanted to help him change.

I became broken for many years until I couldn't take it any longer. The day I finally left would be the last time I woke up to someone hitting me in my face. Something just came over me, I was done. I loaded up my stuff in my car and drove off with nowhere to go. But, I found a way. I found a way to get out. Once I knew I wasn't going back, I felt overwhelmingly free. Why had I been scared of something so uplifting? I was truly proud of myself for leaving, realizing I didn't need to go back and didn't want to.

Now the hard part, I had to accept my freedom could've come much sooner, had I the courage. Now, not only did I hate him, I hated myself. See truth is I could've left at any time. Everyone told me to leave, but I was stuck in a negative relationship of lust. I was fighting to stay alive but dying inside. If you're trying to figure out if you should leave, you probably already know the answer. Don't be afraid, step on the gas and never look back! Money can't buy time. We can easily become prisoners of our own minds. Don't get captured in your thoughts. Stop believing you're weak: know you're strong.

Through growth, I learned to love myself and to forgive. Drop the grudges and love yourself before you ask anyone else to love you. Know yourself. Set standards. Make them very clear at the beginning of your relationship, not two years down the road. I'm talking about before you start dating, while you're just texting or talking, definitely way before sex. You can't allow someone to treat you a certain way, and then expect them to stop. First time something happens, speak up. Let them know this behavior won't be tolerated. If abuse occurs, please know it most likely won't stop. Don't do something one time; you don't want to do again. Remove yourself from this toxic relationship. If not, you'll hurt both of you more than you know. Love isn't supposed to hurt. No matter how much you think you love him, you don't have to stay. Let him go before you let yourself go.

Like me, you should ask yourself, "Is it worth it? Does this relationship make you happy?" If the answer is no, it's not worth it. It's not worth embarrassment from bruises. It's not worth letting your kids see the abuse or lying for him. It's not worth thinking it's all your fault, not his. It's not worth missing the chance at finding your soul mate. It's not worth NOT LIVING. You're not meant to be with him nor him with you. Be better than this. Who cares who's wrong or right in the argument? He's wrong for abusing you. This pattern will repeat. Don't wait for him to change. Don't wait for the right moment. Just fly.

Before I left, I figured out the hard way, I was an enabler. Someone will only do what you let them. Why should he change? Why should he go to work, you already pay for him? Ladies, do not baby your man. He must feel like a man, or you're just setting yourself up. His self-esteem is blown when his woman takes care of him. Throughout history, men have been leaders and providers. Don't take that away. You two are a team. He has his role, and you yours. Now, I'm not saying he should control you. I'm saying he has to play the man's role. If he doesn't know how to take care of himself or his position in life, he's definitely not ready for you. Rethink your commitment. Let him free to find his way. Don't push yourself upon him or push for him to change. One of the worst things you can do is try to force someone to change. Most will do exactly the opposite.

I asked myself was I more afraid of him or me? Reality of it, I was afraid of change. Please, don't be like me. Don't fear all the wonderful things God has in store for you. Change is difficult sometimes, but change can be good. This type of change could be the best thing to ever happen. You won't regret it. Stop trying to make someone love you. Spend more time with the people who have always loved you.

Life passes by before you know it. The only one to truly blame is you. Our relationships with others are a reflection of ourselves. Be surrounded by people who share your same drive. If this means hanging out by yourself do it! You're only as great as your peers. You may have outgrown these people. Don't limit yourself. Don't apologize. It is what it is. They may not be ready for what is coming to you! Don't let them block your blessings. You are important. You are strong. You are beautiful. You are someone special. People love you. Love yourself.

Proverbs 13:20 – He who walks with wise men will be wise, but the companion of fools will suffer harm.

Tanya Cooper

Tanya Cooper is a single mother, entrepreneur, community mentor, and volunteer. She is the mother of three beautiful children; two young adult women, and one teenage son. Tanya's children are the focal points of her stance against mental and physical abuse towards children and women. She has an Associate of Science in Business, and has recently accepted a volunteer position with the Not on My Watch Women Initiative (NOMWWI).

"Why Not Me"

"The greatest gift of forgiving is unadulterated freedom of one's injustices, guilt, shame, and pity."

I have been the strong one in the sight of others; they rely on me to help and encourage them. Who do I have to help me? I have intentionally lived my life in the background of others to ensure they see their full potential, not allowing their current or past experiences, sins, hinder their life journey. I am a firm believer that what is in one's past is truly forgiven by God, through Christ Jesus. And still, the notion of the sea of forgetfulness, never seem to come to fruition for me. I know the scriptures refer to the mind of God and how he sees us through His Son; but I too want to forget several things I have encountered in my life. I can't shake the memories. No matter how much I pray, it still doesn't change the fact that it happened.

I should not have asked my mother about the birds and the bees after watching my favorite show, "Good Times." I found the courage to ask her, but she shot me down with her expressions. She responded in a stern voice, "You don't need to know about that," then walked off. Our relationship was far from the relationship I grew to love from the mother on "The Cosby Show", Claire Huxtable. Mrs. Huxtable spoke to her children about any topic they brought to her. I vowed to do the same for my children to be aware of their experiences in the world, and assure them they were not alone. As a typical teenager, I knew my mother did not love, or care what happened to me. She was too busy fussing and fighting with daddy. Several times I heard my dad say I was not his child, rambling about how light I was in comparison to him. This, among other things, he would say about me, caused me to become angry and bitter towards him. When he was upset with me, he made it very clear, I was a little bitch and would not be shit. Not only did I not talk to my mother about anything, I surely would not talk to my dad.

I was born and raised in East Oakland, California. I lived with both of my parents, and a little brother. I am the eldest child between my mother and father; the third eldest of my father's children. I have two half-sisters, one overseas baby, as my brother and I would joke, and one who lived locally. My town is the home of the Oakland Raiders and the Oakland Athletics (A's team). Our home was so close to the stadium I could hear fans cheer from my front porch at night. There were many nights I would sit outside watching the stars and some days daydreaming among the clouds, wishing I lived somewhere else. Not only was my town known for famous athletes, it had its share of pimps and prostitutes, artists and scholars. It was hard for me to focus on a future when my main goal was to survive the streets.

In my mind, I had no one in my life to rely on, or tell what was happening to me. I bottled all feelings and trusted no one; anger became my comfort and security. I had a best friend who was my way of escape, but I did not share everything with her either. Who would listen to the little fast-tail, hard-headed, seemed to love fighting all the time girl? I am not exactly sure of my age, but a relative, not much older than I, wanted to show me what the birds and the bees were all about. I was by myself, in the kitchen, a door opened and a voice whispering, "Come here". He wanted to show me something, "real quick". While looking at the posters of women plastered everywhere, I asked, "What do you want to show me?" I was uncomfortable and wanted to leave. I said, "If you touch me, I will scream." He walked closer saying, "You came in my room, who they gone believe?" I heard he did this with other relatives, but why me? What did I do to him? He proceeded to kiss me. I felt his spit on my lips, then again he grins. It was impossible to push him off, like a huge stone he would not budge. To show me what a man felt like, he pulled my pants down, and then began touching himself telling me I would like it. While pleading for him to stop, I felt my legs spread open. He attempted to insert his penis, but it did not fit. Perhaps it was the tears falling from my face, or the thoughts of getting caught that caused him to stop, either way, I promised I wouldn't tell if he let me go.

Of course, one would expect to ball up in a corner and cry about what happened. Instead, I sought the attention of other boys; my only criteria were he had to be cute and have money. I realized quickly boys my age would not fit the criteria. The occupations of the guys I fell for ranged from low to high-end drug dealers to want-to-be rappers. I involved myself with guys who did not mind threatening to kill me on the spot or stalk me, if I decided to leave them. "But he loves me", a lie I told myself. Clearly, my perception of love was distorted.

I was naive in my youth. Although my build gave men the illusion that I was a grown woman, I was a little girl, who wanted to have fun, and play. My dad's handyman saw something else in me. While I picked lemons from our huge tree in the backyard that leaned against the house he grabbed my wrist, and pulled me towards him. I did not scream. We were outside, what will he do to me, while my mom is in the house? He said, "In my country, you would be my wife." I looked at him in horror and calmly said, "I am only twelve." I yanked free from him, and then ran to my neighbor's house. I banged on their door frantically; I almost fell on my face when the door opened. I told them what he said and did not go home until he left. Eventually, I told my mom, but I can't recall if she told my dad, because that man would show up to our house like nothing happened. Maybe this was a reason my parent's argued.

The neighbor's daughter and I grew closer. We were both on the chunky side, so we created our own exercise plan. I learned how to make juices, now known as smoothies, and healthy meals. We'd laugh and crack jokes on each other all day. One weekend we must have had too much fun. While getting out of the shower, the bathroom was filled with perfume and scent of powder. She attempted to show me where to spray it, even held my hair up, but her lips pressed against my neck first. She touched my breast gently, and told me I was pretty; unlike my relative, she asked to touch my private area. I realized girls like to show what they know about sex too.

I lived my life as if this incident never happened; she left an imprint of what to expect in the future. Before her, I thought only my boyfriend could be gentle. He was the only boy that showed me guys could be nice and caring. He didn't do what she did, but unlike my relative, he fit. He was tall with perfect chocolate skin tone, dimples you could swim in, and he was the same age. Before my world turned crazy, he was my first love. We could talk about anything, well almost anything that came to mind. Our bond was unbreakable, until my mother moved us to Oklahoma, to escape her abuser, my father.

After moving to Oklahoma, I experienced heartbreaks and spells of depression. I became bitter, felt lonely, and convinced myself that love was not attainable on all levels. Thoughts of suicide visited often, I wanted to end all hurt, until I met a young lady who invited me to church. I am grateful to her and her family for accepting me as I was, wounded. Teaching me what God says about me, his expectations, and the importance of forgiveness, Freedom! What happened to me does not belong to me; instead it is a testament to others on how God will bring us through to our healing space. Forgiveness allowed me to love again, heal broken relationships, and live to witness Gods favor over my family. Trust God, He is faithful.

Two favorite Bible quotes I am reminded of:

- "Greater is he that is in me than he is in the world." (1 John 4:4-6)
- "There is no condemnation to them which are in Christ Jesus…" (Read entire Romans 8).

Jen Cromling

Jen Cromling.grew up in Edmond, Oklahoma andl lives with her husband Josh and their two children Jake and Caroline. She is a Jesus follower and a Major Life Encourager. Her family and God are her top priorities. She has a passion for helping other women find balance and live the life God intended for them. Jen is the Founder of the Oklahoma BOSS Ladies and she loves to find ways to connect powerful women. Her mission is to help women take their life from ordinary to extraordinary.

"Ordinary to Extraordinary"

My name is Jen Cromling. I live in Oklahoma with my husband Josh and our two children. I am praying that my story helps at least one woman see how overcoming is possible. I love the title of the book, A Brilliant Awakening. We often go through life just getting by and never have our own brilliant awakenings. I pray after reading this book you are closer to finding yours.

Most of my life I have fought with anxiety and just an overall feeling of not good enough. I think many of these feelings began in 1994, the year after I graduated high school. I was an athlete in high school and had even been offered a partial scholarship to run track at the University of Central Oklahoma. I was a sprinter in track. I ran with the seniors even as a freshman in high school. Track gave me a lot of confidence in myself. I was shocked when I was offered a partial scholarship to the local community college. Unfortunately, at that time in my life, I didn't understand what a big deal that was and ended up turning down the scholarship. Even though I had no scholarship, I enrolled in school and planned to take out student loans to pay my way through college.

On New Year's Eve in 1994, my life got completely turned upside down. I was at home with my family waiting for my dad to come home to celebrate. We were all going to have dinner and then sit around the TV to watch the New Year ring in. It started to get late, and my dad still wasn't home. This was long before cell phones, so we just sat and waited. The later it got, the more scared we became. It turned out that my dad had chosen New Year's Eve, to run off with his long-time girlfriend. Imagine our devastation. We had no idea that dad even had a girlfriend. He was a family counselor, and he had been having an affair with a colleague. That event impacted me in a major way well into my adult years including the devastation, the rejection, and the aftermath. He just abandoned us all that night. I chose to forgive him long ago, but even through the forgiveness, the pain of how he left never went away. My family has never been the same since.

After that abandonment, I dropped out of college and started working. My life consisted of going to work and going out to the bars after work. I think the only thing that saved my life during those years was that I had given my heart to Jesus in my teens. Even though I was so far away from God, He never left me. Fast forward to 1996, and God sent me a gift, the man that would become my husband. Josh was in college, and he really seemed to have his life together. We were just friends for the longest time until I started to notice I would look forward to seeing him more and more. We eventually started dating, and it was at that point I knew I needed to get my life together. I ended up enrolling in college, and I quit my job at the restaurant. I moved back in with my mom who was always so amazing and willing to help me.

I graduated from college in 2001 with a degree Education and went out into the workforce. I got a great job in Pharmaceutical Sales. Josh and I got married in 2004, and now we have been together for a long time. We now have two amazing children Jake ten and Caroline five. Even though I had this incredible man and this incredible career, my feelings of anxiety and inadequacy did not go away. Then I felt guilty for feeling that way. I was always worried about something. At times, it felt like I could not shut the worry off. I can remember standing in the shower one day, and I thought to myself, I wonder if this is normal? I wondered if I was the only one who lived like this. I felt guilty because I had everything I ever wanted. I had an amazing husband; we had already had our first child, our son Jake. I had a great relationship with my mom, lots of family and friends. I had an amazing career that I really loved. Even though I had all of these things, I still felt inadequate. I knew I wanted to change, but I wasn't sure what to do to help myself.

Four years ago, to make a little extra income, I started a little home based business with a company called Nerium International. At least I thought that is why I started this home-based business. I was working in Pharmaceuticals, I had two little children, and I didn't like to leave the house except for work. I mean why wouldn't I want to start a business in direct sales? Insert sarcasm here. I just felt like it was something I was supposed to do. I ended up having fast success and earned a Lexus, bonuses, trips, and over six figures in additional income for my family. I thought I had done what I set out to do, but I was wrong. There was more than just money and recognition that was in store for me it just took me a while to see it. The company was built around the words, "Make People Better." It was this company that encouraged me to start reading and working in personal development. Over the last two years, I have done so much work on myself. I have been moving towards creating a better me.

It was also two years ago that we started attending Life Church in Edmond, Oklahoma. Pastor Craig Groeschel has made such a huge impact in my life. I have read so many books and listened to so many podcasts there is no way I can give an exact number. Through Life Church, all the personal development and countless hours reading devotionals and praying I finally had a realization. I realized that I never really loved myself. And now I know that this is what God wants for me. God wants us to love ourselves. Proverbs 19:8 says, "To acquire wisdom is to love oneself; people who cherish understanding will prosper." You have to love and value yourself if you ever want to really love others. Through reading and studying, I knew I wanted to grow my relationship with God. I knew that He has an amazing plan for my life, and I knew all I had to do was ask God where He wanted me to be. Through all my reading, I also learned how to speak life. I discovered how all the negative thoughts in my head were getting in the way of my future. I learned you can never feel your way into an action. You are just going to have to do it anyway, even though you don't feel like it. I learned that I am good enough, and I do have a father. I have had Him with me all along. I don't have a father here on earth, but I do in Heaven, and He will never leave me. I learned to fill my mind and thoughts with good things. I know now that what we watch, read, and have around us have a big effect on us.

The girl who was anxious and felt inadequate has changed. I feel powerful and excited for the future. I used to just move through life doing the ordinary. Now I can no longer be ordinary. My relationship with God is too good. I pray every morning for God to show me what He wants me to see, lead my feet where He wants me to go, and use my hands to do His work. I am more present and engaged with my children and husband than ever before. I am a daughter of a wonderful mother and friend to many. I have a fresh perspective and excitement for life. I feel like I have found the secret that so many women are looking for in life. I found the secret to having balance. I found the secret to being my best self. If you could crawl in my head for a second, you would completely understand how unbelievable it is today compared to where I used to be. God has a plan for every one of us. He has it written out, and it is there for you. All you have to do is believe in Him. He will never leave you.

If you have been hurt so bad and abandoned by a family member, you can recover. If anxiety and inadequacy enter your thoughts over and over, you can change that. You have the power to turn off those negative thoughts. You have the power to speak life and change the negative voice in your head that tells you that you are not good enough. If you want to be the best version of yourself, just get moving and remember, you will probably never feel like getting started, but just get started anyway. I believe in you. I am strong, courageous, and firm; I fear not and am not in terror; for the Lord my God who goes with me; He will not fail me or forsake me. - Deuteronomy 31:16

Joan Curtis

Joan Curtis is Fabulous! Just ask her, she will tell you herself! She went on to get her GED and become very successful in her career as an Independent Insurance Agent in the Oklahoma City Metro Area. Joan found she loved the insurance industry because she enjoys educating her clients and the relationships that have developed with the people she serves, "They become my friends and family". Joan has been a frequent public speaker and host for several amazing events in OKC and nationally, speaking on everything from her relationship with God and Family, time managment, relationships and communication, to networking and marketing. Her most passionate topics are the ones that involve stories of her kids and auditory processing disorder, purity and raising her children to know the Lord.

"Teach Them to Forgive"

I love the name of this book, "Brilliant Awakening!" I am not sure if I could be where I am at today if it were not for this thing happening to me. When you experience sexual or mental abuse, you become imprisoned with in your own soul. There is a mental breakdown that happens that puts a part of you to sleep. This part can rule you if you allow it. This book, and these women, that God aligned to write this book are here to become atmosphere changers for our readers. What you have experienced doesn't have to rule you. It is time be awakened to the truth that wants to set you free!

She was the most beautiful thing I have ever seen. My beautiful bouncing baby girl was 6lbs, 14oz of sheer joy and love that I couldn't understand. Never in my life had anything been so perfect and so pure. I knew that I was her mother, and that I had so many things to learn, but one thing I knew for sure was that I would NEVER let happen to her what had happened to me. I was abused, molested and raped. The details of it are not as important to me as how it shaped everything in my life from that point on. Here God had blessed me with this perfect gift, and all I could think of it my severe need to protect her from ever feeling any pain in her life. I was a little girl when all of the abuse started, so little I could always remember it happening. I don't remember my life before because I don't believe there was a life before. My children, of whom she was the first of 4, were going to have something I never had… a fierce protector. You see in my prison that I had created, let's call it my nightmare; I had decided that if I had one mission in life it was to see my children never experience the smallest of pain. My children would have a present and accounted for parent and they would have someone who would defend and advocate for them with my very life if necessary. I don't think all of that is bad, but I do think it is quick to become an idol in my life. My very purpose was to be a mom, and not just a better than mom, but the perfect mom whom would never let anything painful entrap my children in the way I was entrapped.

Fast forward 16 months. I had been married for almost 3 years, and pregnant and breast feeding most of those… my first two are 20 months a part. I had a moment of somewhat skewed clarity one day when my daughter had gotten a little cut that bled. You would have thought she was unfixable the way I carried on about it. She was bleeding!!! Oh MY GOD, she was experiencing physical pain! A neighbor showed me my crazy when I was in tears and asked if she had a Band-Aid. "Joan, she is fine, it is just a little scratch! You better pull yourself together; being a kid is about skinned knees and pain!" My daughter wasn't crying, but I was a wreck! That is when I decided maybe I am a little off balance in the way I am handling my life. It sounds crazy right, who wouldn't want to protect their precious baby, but I was overboard. It was my very obsession to protect my kids even from my husband, any male person in our family, and most of all from strangers!

I remember that day very well. It was a cool spring day and I was about 7 months pregnant with my second. I had decided to go back to counseling to deal with my abuse as I was sure now that all was not put away as I had previously thought. When you have been abused in any form it can become such second nature to protect yourself, but you can't help but have it spill out in a lot of different unhealthy ways. I call it bleeding, when something affects every part of your life, and you can't stop it. You need more than just a Band-Aid. You need a complete healing! Just when you think it is about to heal, it is like a scab that gets reopened and reopened over and over again. I just hadn't seen it as clearly as I did with my daughter getting cut. I was seriously making my kids my idols and to my detriment becoming that helicopter mom and can hinder them more than I can help them. This had affected my marriage as well. I loved my husband, but he was a man, and that meant I couldn't fully trust him. I have been married now for 20 years, but the abuse had become like scabs in many facets of our marriage over the years. But I digress… I was sure that there was something I needed to deal with, so I went back to my trusted counselor Robert.

Proudly I sat there. Sure of myself and ready to deal with this once and for all. See, I didn't have a real problem, just little ones that just needed a little attention and then I could get back to my life. In the conversation with Robert I had proudly and almost defiantly stated "This will never happen to my kids, because they have me!"

"Really." said Robert. "Yes, really! I am there with my child day in and day out. I know everyone who comes in contact with her, and I am in complete control!" I said.

"Wow!!" he said. The room became smaller in that moment, as Robert extended his two hands forward palms facing upward like the scales of justice. "Whom does God love more, you or the one who abused you?"

WHAT? I know there was a right answer here, but obviously God loves me more right? NO… We all know the answer to that. "Neither." I said.

"So whose free will can God take yours or your abusers?" He said very calmly.

"Neither…' I said very meek and quietly. I don't like how this is going… I will be honest, I could feel the anger start inside of me. That uncomfortable feeling, the fight or flight response, was coming on like a tidal wave.

"You can't stop someone from choosing to sin against your daughter." He said.

What the hell is he talking about?

How dare him!

I have never felt anger like this in my life. Why would God give me these perfect children, my daughter, and what was about to be my son, and not give me the ability to protect them against this ever happening to them. The thought that I as a mother was powerless all over again against my abuser or their abuser was completely unacceptable. I felt fire in my heart, and my eyes felt the heat from that fire. I got up and said "NO! You can't tell me that I cannot protect my daughter!'

He just sat back and looked at me very patiently and very lovingly fatherly voice said, "That is exactly what I am telling you."

To say I stormed out was an understatement.

I don't remember the drive home. All I remember was walking into my home and my husband saw me. He was holding our 18 month old girl on his hip. He saw me and turned her away from me and held up his hand like a crossing guard "STOP! You need to be alone, you look angry"

Little did I know I was grunting from anger. He said that when he looked at me all he could think was to protect her from me. Protect her from ME!

I walked upstairs and began to scream at God. I know God can handle cussing, because my vocabulary was 3 parts cussing and 1 part regular appropriate language.

"HOW DARE YOU GOD! HOW DARE YOU TELL ME I CANNOT PROTECT HER?" I was exposed and vulnerable in ways I had never been before, and that is saying a lot from someone whose first memories are of sexual abuse. Tears streaming down my face and screaming inaudible groaning... "NOOOOOO! AUGHHHHHHHH!" I was completely broken before God. Raw, unedited, and broken, I felt like Satan had won the battle, when all of a sudden God spoke to me.

God may not speak to everyone audibly, but I will tell you it was as clear as day. "Teach them to forgive." I felt the arm of the Holy Spirit reach into my heart through my throat and literally still my beating heart for just enough time to remove the pain I had felt from being abused. I felt like I was choking on a forearm. God touched me in a way that healed the bleed. He reached into my soul and forever changed me. It was a miraculous healing. The Holy Spirit reminded me that Jesus died for ALL sin…even the sin that happened to me. I was restored. That day God was my Heavenly Father who CAN protect me from all that pain. I just never turned to Him like that. In weeks to come and years to follow, I have never once cried over my abuse. It was removed from me as if it never happened. I began to read the word. I began to speak God's word over my kids and prepare them for struggles in life because it says in 1 Peter "In all this you greatly rejoice, though now for a little while you may have had to suffer grief in all kinds of trials".

As for my children, there are 4 of them now, 2 girls and 2 boys. I have made it my purpose to teach them what Jesus did for them. The entire purpose of the cross was and is forgiveness. When you forgive those who trespass against you, you are the one that is freed. I cannot stop my children from sinning, or allowing themselves to be in a place where they are sinned against. I pray it never happens to them the way it has happened to so many. But I do know that God has healed me! I do know my life it on course for great purpose which Satan meant to derail all those years ago, but God will use for good for me as I love him and am called according to His purpose! As I write this, some of my children are grown and living the fruit of this day. My daughter is pure, and chaste, and completely submitted to God in her own relationship. No she wasn't abused, but she does have trials and tribulations of her own. They all will, and I am okay with that. I serve a God that is bigger than any circumstance. I have forgiven and I am free.

Deuteronomy 7:19 says "You saw with your own eyes the great trials, the signs and wonders, the mighty hand and outstretched arm, with which the Lord your God brought you out. The Lord your God will do the same to all the peoples you now fear."

God gave me an outstretched arm, and He can do the same for you. I will continually pray for you, and ask that you pray for me. Awaken!

Julie Daugherty

Julie Daugherty owns A Royal Secret, Hair Studio where she proudly has 1 Cor 9:25 on the front window of her salon. She also is a Paul Mitchell educator, founder of Ohio Boss Ladies, and an Independent Partner with Nerium International. Just Julie is a wife,mother, Mamaw and girl who loves God and wants to live life to the fullest and help as many people as she can along the way!! Julie lives in Dover, Ohio with her husband Chad.

"Know You Are Fearfully & Wonderfully Made"

Hi there, I'm Just Julie, a girl just like most of you, probably. My childhood could have been better but could have been worse. I had a strict, hardworking dad and a very religious mom. What I took from it made me who I am today. So, today I am a 50-year-old mom to Morgan (32), Dane (27), and Brock (15). I am also Mamaw Julie to Landon (10), Liliyana (eight), Liam (two) and Noah (seven months). I grew up in a very small town Midvale, Ohio, and after high school, getting married, and spending a year in Germany, I went to Cosmetology school. I worked in a couple of salons, managed Regis Hairstylist for over 12 years, and then opened my own salon almost 11 years ago. I also met my husband, Chad, in that same timeframe, and that's how I got my bonus son, Brock.

I'm not going to go into my childhood, and as a mother myself, I know we do a lot of the wrong things for the right reasons. I also know when talking to your parents and then your own kids, we remember things differently, or maybe it's just how we took things? My perspective growing up in little Pentecostal churches was if it was fun, you were going to burn in Hell for eternity. My dad didn't go to church unless it was a holiday, but he was strict, and my brother and I knew we better behave. So, I was always carrying the guilt with me, and I made plenty of mistakes, so trust me, the guilt stayed with me a while. Getting pregnant and having my daughter at 18 really started the life of shame and guilt, and when the marriage didn't work out, that feeling was multiplied. My second marriage was to a preacher's son who I thought for sure was from God. We had a son, but the marriage fell apart, so more shame, more guilt!! The worse thing is that even with abuse and cheating, you still try and keep it together; you feel so embarrassed, but you can't make people love you; you can't make them stay. Trust me; I watched all the fairytales; nobody gets married planning on getting divorced. Every girl wants her "Happily Ever After!"

My mom once told me as an adult, "Your dad works like three men. I didn't work, so the house was always clean, and most meals were homemade, and you think you can work like your dad, and take care of your kids and house like you don't have a job. It's unrealistic expectations that can never possibly be made." but I sure tried!! Despite all that I felt like a colossal failure!! I just knew I was letting my parents down and setting a horrible role model for my kids!! So, to make up for that, I just kept working a ton of hours and tried to keep my house clean and meals cooked. I would have my kids super involved at church, every sport they wanted to play, plus extra camps, dance, karate, and anything else, and never miss a party or a program. As you can imagine, this was not good at all for my health, and my first surgery at the age of seven was just the beginning of a lifelong history of kidney stones, stomach problems, and even cancer several times. I was a total mess. And then a few years ago, with my Awesome Chad and a chance to slow down with work, I thought I was finally going to be able to have a nice life, so WHY would all these awful memories start destroying my peace? I was diagnosed with PTSD. You can't just try to ignore things happening, push memories away, and try and just work like crazy because as soon as you slow down, you're going to have to deal with it. The abuse, rejection, and shame had a medical hold on me. I never slept, was always so emotional, and was just all over the place when I was trying to talk or do anything. When you're operating on guilt and shame, you try and do it all by yourself; you avoid relationships and situations where you think you'll be judged, and you try and overdo for everyone. It's like you think you have to do, give, or buy things for people to like you. And I could NEVER say no, that meant I was bad, a bad friend, a bad person, a bad Christian.

Thank God not too long after this, I went to a hair show in Columbus, Ohio, and met Jen, this precious girl from Oklahoma. She introduced me to Nerium International, and her friendship and this company have changed my life. Not just because of the money, free trips, and getting to drive a Lexus for free, but Nerium partnered with Signum Bioscience out of Princeton University who developed EHT, this little brain pill (supplement) that lets me sleep, stay focused, and relieve anxiety issues I'd dealt with for years. We don't meet people by chance; God knows what He's doing.

I can tell you for the fact that a God has blessed me with some pretty amazing people in my life, family. At the age of seven, I and my lifelong BFF, Michelle, both moved to Midvale, and we have had 43 crazy amazing years of friendship. She pretty much lived in my house growing up, and even though we would move around a little, I even was out of the country for a bit, we always remained the best of friends. We met Kirk when we were 15 years old, and they would go on to get married, but because I had no luck in that department, he would become "Our Husband." From coming to fix my furnace in the middle of the night to being the one to say Chad and I needed to meet, he was there. The four of us would also go on an amazing cruise together for their 25th anniversary and would have also traveled many places all over the world, but he was killed on his motorcycle, and he will be missed by so many of us until the day we die!! I've been blessed by too many amazing friends to list, but I sure hope and pray they all know how much they mean to me. I've also attended some great churches and groups through the years. We currently attend Legacy Church in New Philadelphia, where we'd love to have you visit if you ever get to our little part of Ohio.

Another life changing group for me would have to be Propel… Cassie, the girl who got it going in our area, is also a preacher's kid with a personality just like me, I had no idea that she was going to help me break out of a 50-year lie that Satan had convinced me of. Just Julie had seen herself as a girl full of shame, guilt, and embarrassment for most her life. I thought God had to be so disappointed in me. And, how could He forgive me when I couldn't forgive myself? I was positive He wanted me to be the opposite of the girl I was. I wanted to be that sweet little quiet girl, but for as long as I could remember I was the loud, nonstop talking girl I hated myself for being. But, when Cassie stood at the front of the room, she would list all her strengths: friendly, talkative, didn't know a stranger. I mean every single thing she saw as a positive, I was embarrassed about. I will NEVER forget her smile when she answered me when I told her how I felt, she said. "Girl, people have always been trying to get me to sit down and be quiet, THAT'S NOT HOW GOD MADE ME!" And, all night I thought about that, and even the next morning, I thought about a poster my mom had when I was younger that said: "I know I'm special because God doesn't make junk!" Think about that. God made every one of us, so being ashamed of how I was, was saying God didn't know what He was doing. Then, I went to a big Nerium meeting, and driving home afterward I started thinking about all the people who came up to me asking questions and commenting on things I had said that were so helpful to them. That's a pretty amazing feeling, so we need to thank God, and remember we are fearfully and wonderfully made. So yes, I'm loud, even when people don't see me, they HEAR me. They know my voice, and you need to hear your voice, because, "The voice you hear and believe, is the future you will experience."

LaTaye Davis

LaTaye Davis is an electrifying speaker, author, creative brand strategist who seeks to improve the rights of women. Her company Stilettos in the City Brand Management offers brand management, brand development, and business start-up/sustainment for community leaders, politicians, and speakers. LaTaye Davis, LLC, focuses on systems which enhance and improve work-life balance. LaTaye also hosts events which link women in the state of Mississippi to spark entrepreneurship, collaboration, and education. As an Army veteran, she has led, inspired, and helped heal military personnel, family members, and government employees while serving at Walter Reed Army Medical Center, the White House Medical Unit, and the Pentagon just to name a few. LaTaye obtained her Bachelor degree while balancing her career and single motherhood. Her experience in various industries such as retail and state/federal government enable her to be able to effectively navigate in diverse environments.

"Visible Camouflage"

Maybe it was the way my BDUs moved as I marched in formation or the gracious smile I gave to my battle buddies as I walked past them. Could it have been the way my PT shorts hugged my butt as I did my daily exercise or how I walked in confidence and acted silly with my medical battle buddy? Was it my southern drawl that made me way too familiar to him or my brushing off of his suggestive comments that he took as interest and consent? It's in these moments I look at what happened to me and I feel helpless, confused, and torn.

Per an article published in The Military Times on May 5, 2016 "The military received more than 6,000 reports of sexual assaults last year, but only a small fraction, about 250, led to a court-martial and conviction for a related crime, according to a new Pentagon report. The military received more than 6,000 reports of sexual assaults last year, but only a small fraction, about 250, led to a court-martial and conviction for a related crime, according to a new Pentagon report."

I am LaTaye Davis and I'm a victim of sexual assault.

I remember watching an episode of Law and Order: SVU where its' lead character, Detective Benson, had to deal with (or refuse to deal with) an assault she experienced at the hands of an obsessed stalker. Standing amongst her peers she was unable to come to terms with what had happened to her and attempted to function in a "business as usual" manner. I recognize, way too well, that unwillingness to be viewed as weak or powerless.

Then, as if God knew I needed to see myself in someone else, I was watching "Couples Therapy" and was taken aback by Renee's inability to speak about being violated by her husband. She couldn't say the word...you know that word that is as bad as the scarlet letter. It is the same word that stamps you (as most of us wrongfully believe) as weak, oppressed, and unable to protect ourselves. That word Renee could not use to describe herself (and neither could I) and I realized in that moment myself as well, was the word "victim".

I never thought I would have this word attached to me. Growing up, I witnessed domestic violence in my home. At any point, regardless of time of day, I could easily be awakened by loud voices, arguing, and/or physical altercations. Not only was it in my home but within my extended family as well. It's strange how I experienced it so much that it became a part of my life. Although it was embarrassing at times, especially when I knew my friends heard my parents arguing or physically fighting, it became my norm.

Because of my past, I vowed never to experience what I had seen my mother, and other women in my life, deal with.

I made promises to myself. I said I would never allow someone to physically hurt me. Watching so many women in my life get abused by men who were supposed to "love" them caused me to put a barrier to protect myself.

So how did I, the strong woman...independent woman...a soldier...put me in a position to get raped? My mind blocked it out because "we" don't allow things like this to happen to us and "we" never lose control of a situation. I was trained to assess situations and identify potential threats. I think I let my guard down because this would never happen in the environment I was in.

While attending a military training course I was raped. You would never think during a course, surrounded by some of the Army's best soldiers, I would find myself being sexually assaulted. I had gotten to know a lot of the non-commissioned officers who were attending the course with me and never felt fearful or threatened at any point. I was surrounded by the cream of the crop; the best soldiers in the Army. On the day I answered my door, in the barracks, I didn't think I would be raped. I can remember his hands touching me and I laughed it off to ease the vibe I was starting to feel. What started off as slight flirting and joking (or at least I thought he was joking) about how "I couldn't handle him" led to me being forced on my bunk, pinned under him struggling to keep my shorts up as he fought me to get them down. My strength was no match to his. It seemed the more I pushed the more control he gained. There was so much intent in his actions and I couldn't figure out what to do about it. He was breathing in my face and it was obvious to me he came to my room with a purpose. His body weight suffocated me. I was scared, confused, and absent. I was absent because at some point I left my own body and went to a place, in my mind, where sex was about love and respect. I'm In that moment I created an alternate reality where I was loved and a man wanted me and only me. I realize I did that in an attempt to take back control of something I had no control over.

What do you do in that moment? Fear, denial, confusion were all circulating in my mind at the same time. I remember being too proud to make any noise...I didn't want anyone to hear or know what was going on. After he finished I did nothing. I sat on the side of the bed as he pulled back up his pants, made a stupid joke, and walked out of the room. I didn't go shower because I believed people would be able to see "it" on me. I sat on the side of the bed and tried to figure out how I could continue with training. Not because I was angry but because I was ashamed. I knew it would be all over me and I would be looked at as "loose" or "easy." I blamed myself because it was easier than speaking up. I feared if I mentioned it to anyone it would make my time there worse and permanently hurt my career. Because he was connected, was viewed as one of the favorites in the course, and was very outspoken I convinced myself it was in my best interest to keep my mouth shut. The thought of standing in formation and having everyone looking at me as if I was the "trouble starter" scared me most. I was scared of reprisal if I did file a report. I didn't want to be the NCO who was raped during school and have that follow me for the rest of my career. I didn't want to be the one who everyone whispered about in formation or when I walked into the room. It was my fear of what OTHERS would say and think that led me to victimize myself. I stood in formation the next day and behaved as if nothing happened. I never said anything.

My "alter ego" stepped in; I shut myself off from my feelings, put back on my uniform and continued to "soldier" on. I couldn't allow anyone to see me as weak or damaged.

When I thought of what happened to me I justified the incident by blaming myself. It was easier for me to say I failed to keep myself safe than blame my offender. I couldn't grasp nor deal with the idea of being unable to protect myself. Remember, I had seen women in my life who were unable to protect themselves.

I convinced myself I must have sent out signals which made this person thinking I wanted to have sex with him. I know I said "No" over and over again but why didn't he care? Although I said no it still happened. Did I really mean "yes?" Were my past acts of promiscuity the reason I was violated? I never blamed him as much as I blamed myself. Somehow, I blocked the rape out of my mind because I couldn't stop blaming myself.

I want to be clear and say the military is an amazing organization which provided me with experiences I would have probably never had experienced in my lifetime. Yet, within the ranks there are issues of sexual discrimination and assault. The tough part is eliminating incidences such as these. What are you to do when your superior or a peer becomes the aggressor? What happens when you're sexually violated and you fear reprisal or humiliation? Who do you really turn to when someone takes from you as if he/she owns you and you are left feeling you have no recourse.

Women join the military for many reasons. I pray every day for myself and for the women who have been raped by a man who they believed they could trust. I stand hand in hand with you as you begin to deal with being violated and disrespected. I hear your frustration at being deployed, being given extra shifts, or being given orders to relocate because you denied the advances of a superior leader (or even worse was raped and then blackballed). There aren't any words to explain the environment we have been subjected to.

To find peace I have to tell myself "It's not about what's done to me but about how I deal with what's been done to me." For so many years I presented myself by what others defined me as. I acted out because of what had been done to me because I was unable to speak up, effectively, for myself. Today, I am able to accept that I am a rape victim. It doesn't make me weak, oppressed, nor less than. It makes me strong and willing to face head on the cards I have been dealt. I'm able to love and live.

To every woman, especially my battle buddies who have suffered sexual abuse/assault while serving our country, I want to encourage you to keep loving, keep trying, and keep speaking. Your life has purpose and your voice can save another woman. Together, we are a force to stand on the frontline to protect the rest of our sisters. You're stronger than you know and your story is more valuable than you can see.

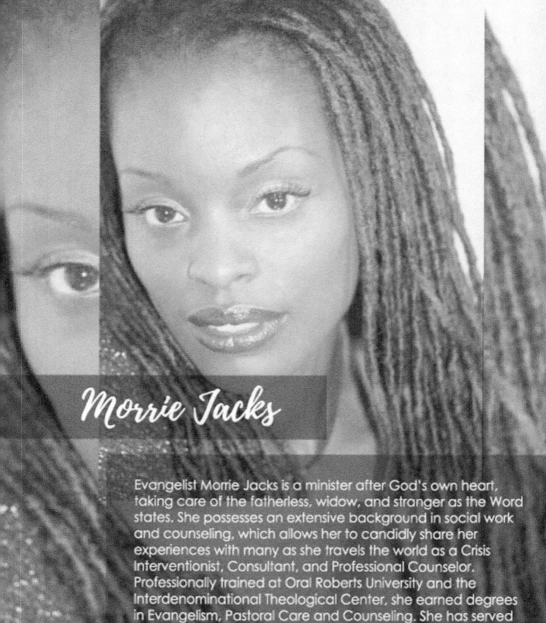

Morrie Jacks

Evangelist Morrie Jacks is a minister after God's own heart, taking care of the fatherless, widow, and stranger as the Word states. She possesses an extensive background in social work and counseling, which allows her to candidly share her experiences with many as she travels the world as a Crisis Interventionist, Consultant, and Professional Counselor. Professionally trained at Oral Roberts University and the Interdenominational Theological Center, she earned degrees in Evangelism, Pastoral Care and Counseling. She has served as Associate Pastor for St. James C.O.G.I.C in Toledo, OH and the Creative Director for the Girls' Teen Summit based in Tulsa, OK.

"No More Silence"

I am Morrie L. Jacks this is a part of my story, not the whole nor the completion. I was in the family room the den; I had fallen asleep on the sofa bed while watching television, when I felt my big cousin press his weight on me to the point I could not move and could barely breathe trying to say, "Stop! Stop! You are hurting me." My face was pressed into the corner of the couch, and my panties pulled to the side so hard and tight to the point of the elastic burning my inner thigh crease my skin was cut, burnt, and swollen. Then there was the feeling of sliminess on the back of my legs behind and thighs. I remember feeling grossed out like there was snot on me. I was afraid to move and crying because the side of my inner leg and thigh was burning and hurting. Then I became totally confused and upset when he uttered the words "Look what you did." Yes, he blamed me as if it was all my fault as if I caused him to hurt me. I was ashamed and heartbroken.

I was a child; a flat chested, no curves girl without even breast buds! I wore cornrows and multi-color beads in my hair and I was still wearing patent leather shoes and lace ankle socks on Sunday. I was an impressionable child. This was my older cousin whom I loved so very much. He was cool, one of my protectors. He was always teaching me how to skate backward or practicing his slow dance skate routine. Hmmmmmh! Shaking my head as think back, he was grooming me all the time. I looked up to him. He was living at my Big Mama's house because he started getting into trouble hanging with the wrong crowds in the Bay Area. I grew up around him. I didn't even know I had to be careful because we were first cousins. He betrayed me and destroyed my innocence.

"FAMILY!" as Big Mama would say about her grandchildren whenever we did not get along. This was the beginning of me really fighting inwardly and outwardly. I was really me fighting to take back my honor, respect and dignity. If I felt the need to protect myself or loved ones, I would get into fights - physical altercations! My friends would say she loves hard and is loyal to a fault, but she doesn't scare well! During those times in my rage and wrath, I couldn't believe my heart was actually breaking and shattering pieces of me and my faith in love.

I believe myself to be a very giving and trusting person. However, I know to receive trust you must trust yourself. I have found it a struggle at times to trust my own heart when it comes to men and love. I had a fear of it not being right or just another flutter of hope. At times I was hoping in my heart, asking myself is HE safe? Is he REALLY safe to LOVE? I desired in my heart to fully submit just once in my life. I wanted to fully understand and know that he had me, my back and my front so that I would know I was safe too. Often I have felt gullible, scared, unsure, and alone in my perception. I have felt and have been totally humiliated at times. I was so far off. Guarding my heart is a behavior I was taught from my Big Mama and my Mother. They would often say those exact words to me, "Guard Your Heart". Put your trust in no man, only in God!" and they would follow up with, "There is no good thing in this flesh!" The emphasis was always on "Guard Your Heart." Between listening to them and growing in my womanhood, that inner space in every woman, I really began to hear them. I listened beyond their words with a painful understanding. I know these things were learned due to being molested and raped by an older cousin in the safest place I knew outside of the church, my Big Mama and Big DD's house, my sanctuary.

My grandfather is the late Bishop E. E. Cleveland Sr., and my grandmother is the late Mother Matilda Cleveland. Together they pastored Ephesians COGIC Northern and Southern California as well as presiding over the Southern California 2nd Jurisdiction COGIC. My Big Mama and Big DD were larger than life. Most of my relatives are larger than life as I think about it. Some have had the honor to serve by their sides in their local churches, communities, and across this nation and many foreign countries. I wanted to be just like my grandparents, as did many that knew them. My grandmother was a sweet, beautiful woman of few words but great actions, gifted to bring together family and hold them together. He was SWAG anointed by God to the 10th degree and was nicknamed "The Globe Trotter" for his mission trips and evangelism. They taught me to love and honor God, which has been the glue that has kept mind together and heart intact most of life. Truly, my testimony is "But for God's grace it could be me!" I could have lost my life or I could be strung out on drugs living a life of defeat and depression. I am so grateful for God's mercies which has preserved me and filled my heart and mind with inner peace.

Molestation and rape leave marks and deep emotional scars that you cannot see with the natural eye. It creates levels of vulnerability that are often silently damaging one's self-worth. In realizing these painful effects, I began creating safe zones in my mind. Many times, I felt alone while being in a room full of people. I did not want something to be taken from me so I had to "guard my heart" against those who would not ask but take from me.

There are physical and spiritual implications that had to be dealt with as well generational cycles that I had to defeat. I was not aware of these types of things as a child or even a young woman. I was starting to see that men had a feeling of entitlement. If they wanted it, they could just take it. I see submission as a gift. For a woman to be willing to give herself is a gift of mind, body, and spirit and should be treated as a precious treasure. I expected no less. I knew I could not allow my cousin to destroy my destiny; as he had often tried belittling me in our community and attacking my character on every end. He was trying to make himself appear to be more than what he was which is nothing more than a child molester, rapist, liar, adulterer, and whore monger. It became a very lonely feeling, but I smiled and was strong on the outside with a silent screams and tears on the inside.

It was not until my college days at Oral Roberts University that I truly began to take back my authority as a woman with feelings of empowerment as I started to activate the gifts and anointing upon my life. My grandparents and mother are still the greatest example of this in my life. I saw strength, compassion, love, respect, honor, and all I ever wanted coming from them. I did not understand why I did not have the same experiences. I was experiencing very violent acts because I was not able to protect myself. I was being taken by force, which was causing pain, hurt, anger and mental anguish.

Now I can truly say to young women that there is power in the midst of one's pain and silent screams. I was determined not to be a victim but a victor! Being a statistic was simply unacceptable on all levels. I grew up praying and fasting, and I knew only God could heal my bruised places and turn each scar of the heart into brilliant and radiant stars that would shine for me. God is granting me opportunities to be a testimony of how He refreshes, restores, and revives the heart, mind, and body. There is something so awesome about walking in authority in places where your head should be hung low, and your self-esteem and self-worth should be shattered.

Now I'm able to minister wholeness and healing as I look so many women in the eye who have suffered the painful violence of being molested, raped, tormented, and silenced. I am so grateful to my Lord Jesus Christ to have an opportunity to tell my story and own it with great conviction! I am thankful to operate in an anointing of deliverance over this vicious tormentor called rape molestation and isolation. I won't be silent anymore!

Dr. Christina R. Kirk

Dr. Christina R. Kirk is a woman after God's heart. After dropping out of high school, Christina earned a Bachelor's of Arts from historic Fisk University and Juris Doctorate from University of Tulsa, School of Law. Christina currently teaches middle school. Christina is also Municipal Court Judge for the City of Langston, Oklahoma. Christina's dedication to the youth is immeasurable. She has received several community service and leadership awards. She encourages women and girls about the importance of self and education. In dedication to her mentor, Dr. Olgesby, Christina founded Prep U in 2009 to empower and support young ladies to a life of good success through college preparation and mentorship. In 2013, Christina honored her mentor and shared her story of inspiration and overcoming obstacles on the Steve Harvey Show. Christina is the proud mother of, Déja Kirk. In her spare time, she loves to travel and shop.

"Five Little Words"

"I can't do this anymore," he said. And with that one sentence a family relationship and what I thought was a healthy marriage, almost two decades old, ceased to exist. One would think that was the end of the story. One would be wrong. It was only the beginning of a five-year journey of self-discovery rotating through a circular path of healing, forgiveness, acceptance, depression, pain, pseudo-victories, and finally, life again. That one sentence changed my life forever.

So many questions ran through my mind as I sat in disbelief and dismay. The resounding "I can't do this anymore" playing over and over in my head. That one sentence generated so many questions. God, why me? What do you do when your idea of being blessed by God is no longer a reality? What do you do when you feel like the God you have loved your whole life has abandoned you? How do you fight on and push through when the desire to fight eludes you? How do you pray to the very God you are mad at for allowing you to feel such pain? What do you do when there are more questions than answers?

I grew up in church. I was not a drug-to-church child. I was the one who went to church even if my mom and grandmother did not go. I called the church bus line and dressed eagerly to get to church. I sang in the youth and mass choirs (although I am quite tone deaf) gospel songs about how I've come this far by faith, there's no greater love than a man who would lay down his life for a friend, and Jesus is a friend of mine. I believed the songs I sang. Honestly, I went to church to see my friends and have fun with them; but, while there hanging with friends, I learned about a God who loves me. I did not know what that love truly meant when I learned about it. That love planted itself firmly in my heart.

Knowing God loves me and knowing the pain of "I can't do this anymore" did not reconcile in my brain. I could not comprehend a love that hurt beyond measure. Anger, confusion, and a bitter disdain for a God I loved and whom I thought loved me quickly turned into my own version of "I can't do this anymore."

I screamed in despair from the depths of my very soul to the God I once revered with every ounce of my being. I turned my face from Him and hardened my heart. I purposely did those things I knew were not pleasing to Him. I dated men I never would have dated before. I did not go to church. I selfishly pursued things to bring about a false sense of pleasure. I gave not only my body but my spirit over to idol gods - men, possessions, experiences, money, etc. I think in the back of my mind I wanted to hurt God because I felt God was hurting me.

I was defeated by life. I was defeated by what I thought life would be. I felt my whole life of serving a merciful God and living a "good" life was in vain. This defeat spiraled into depression. I hurt on a level that I was unable to process the pain, and it left a void my self-destructive behavior could not fill. My mental pain turned to physical pain. I was sick all the time. I did not want to do anything I once did. Anything that reminded me of the life I had before those five little words came out of his mouth was on my list of never to be done again, no matter how much I once enjoyed it. I really was not punishing him. I was punishing myself. He moved forward with love and life and there I stood, stuck in one spot...mad...hurt...depressed...blaming God.

God is big enough to handle my blame. He is big enough to allow me to be mad at Him. He is big enough for me to turn my back and yet He never turned His back on me. I like to think it was the prayers of so many stored up for me for such a time as this, seeds planted as I went to church to see my friends, and words of songs I sang off key that reminded me of this fact. They kept me from drifting too far away from the tenets of my foundation. It took all of that and then some because I was done with God, but God was not done with me.

After months of feeling sorry for myself and being mad at God, I emerged slowly from my cocoon of self-destruction. I began to realize all the tangibles I chased to give me moments of escape, from pain and hurt I felt, really did not do what I needed them to do. I made myself worse. Each night of amazing sex ended with a morning of unbearable regret and shame. Each weekend shopping trip not only ended with credit card debt but also with buyer's remorse. My overindulgences ended with great emptiness and I was still alone. Each day I did not get out of bed and do what I needed to do, only made the to-do list longer and created more self-emotional mutilation. This was not the life I dreamt of, just like I had not dreamt of life without my family intact. I traded one failed dream at someone else's hands for another failed dream at my own hand. This had to stop.

Those same five little words took on a whole new meaning. I can't do this anymore. I can't do this *to myself* anymore. I cannot continue *to hurt me.* I can't keep circling in pain. I just cannot. New questions arose. How do I get off this rollercoaster? How do I heal myself? Can I be healed? Will God take me back? Where to start?

I started where I was - at the bottom; both figuratively and literally. I was sitting on the bathroom floor of my apartment crying liking a newborn in need of picking up and swaddling. In a way, I was a newborn. I started over. I had to do it because I had no choice. I could not keep going in the same direction. I needed the God I learned about to pick me up, wrap me in His love, hold me, reassure me everything was going to be okay. I needed Him to remind me I am His child before I was anyone's ex-wife. And you know what? He did just that.

In that moment, verses I learned many years before came rushing to my memory all with a newfound sense of understanding. Pressing forward and forgetting those things behind me while understanding there is no condemnation. Waking up to new mercies became life and life more abundantly. Peace surpassed all understanding. He was made strong in my weakness. Moreover, after I suffered a little while He restored, established, strengthened, and encouraged me for His sake.

God and I had many moments like this over the next few years. I would think I was over the hurt and pain and no longer mad at God; then I would have a memory or see something that would bring a flood of emotions not yet properly processed rushing back to me propelling me back into my woe-is-me-ness. I would sit there alone, or so I thought, for a while not knowing God was there, too, patiently waiting for me to see He had not left me. He was still right there with me. Then I would be back to that newborn in need again. God never said, "I told you so." He simply picked me up, cradled me in His arms, loved on me, and reassured me of to whom I belonged.

Eventually, I learned to forgive. Not forgive someone else, but forgive myself. I learned to accept me. I learned to accept where I am in life. No, it is not the life I planned for myself. No, it is not the storybook romance I always wanted to share with my grandchildren one day, but it is MY life. I learned forgiving and accepting me were quintessential to my healing. I learned I wanted to be whole. I needed to be whole.

While on and off the rollercoaster, I had a teenage daughter looking to me for her definition of strength. I am her outline of how to handle the tough and hard times when they come because they will come. She needed to know the source of my strength. She needed to know the God to whom I cried *"I can't do this anymore!"* She needed to know that one sentence changed my life forever but it did not end my life; it simply started a new chapter.

Dervina Knowles

Dervina 'Nicole Narae' Knowles' is a public speaker, youth mentor, multi-media journalist, and radio host. She was born in Miami, FL. Nicole is the founder of Beautifully Flawed, which teaches women to get rid of self critical thoughts about themselves by developing self confidence through sisterhood, resources, and interactive workshops. She is passionate about helping women build healthy self images, positive relationships, and prosperous businesses. She currently lives in Fort Lauderdale, FL, and spends most of her free time shopping at thrift stores and lounging on the beach. Her mantra is "Breakthroughs & Boss Moves".

"A Clean Sweep for My Soul"

I am disgusted with the "sweeping things under the rug" mentality, so I have made a commitment to talk about it so not only are we aware but we hold each other accountable. I learned how to consciously release what bothers me. I fought to be the woman I am right now. I love me, and I am freaking awesome. I am fearfully and wonderfully made even after I was molested by David Charles Coker, a man I called my grandfather, my grandmother's husband, my step-grandfather. I decided to share my story and become a first-time co-author because I know there's someone out there struggling with how to deal with all the emotional bondage that comes with sexual and physical abuse. The goal is that you realize that you are not alone and get some tips on how to start living your best life.

I am dedicating this chapter to women and young girls who may be dealing with the guilt, shame, and hush-mouth epidemic of sexual, physical, or mental abuse and illness. I pray that you find the courage to speak up and speak out about the effects of abuse. I pray that you find true peace within yourself to unapologetically and confidently move on.

I am also dedicating this chapter to my younger biological sisters: Vandera, Alyssia, and Amanda. As your older sister, I don't think either one of you really understood my transitions when we were kids. It was not always easy to get along with me at some points, but I think we made it through an unbreakable bond called sisterhood. Now I know you all understand life through similar views as each of you has experienced your own trials and triumphs to womanhood. I only set out to encourage you to be your best self as young women. I am so proud of all three of you and thank you for loving me unconditionally. Cheers to sisterhood.

I would like to acknowledge the man that God is sending my way as my Boaz, my best friend, my honey bunches of oats, my Hershey's kisses through the good, bad, and ugly --- my future husband. Dear Husband, whoever you are, and wherever you are in the world right now, I pray that sharing my truth is a is not a demise as your wife but a mark of bravery to heal my broken wounds before submitting my heart to you. Thank you for still finding me worthy as your Queen while I share an intimate part of my life with the world. Love, your amazing Soon-To-Be-Wife.

The reality is growing up in an island household we had this understanding that what happened with our immediate family and in our home stayed between us. I would like to take a moment to acknowledge my parents, who kept this secret from most the family members to protect me. I just want you to know that you didn't do anything wrong as parents and you all handled the situation the best way you could to help me. You all are incredible individuals, and I am forever grateful to have you as my parents. Lastly, I want to dedicate this chapter to my sheros who are my guardian angels, my paternal and maternal grandmothers, the late Alice Knowles and the late Viola Coker.

Here's some quick background information. I was born with a birth defect called Spina Bifida and my family refers to me as a "Miracle Baby." My parents divorced, and both remarried quickly. They are still happily married to different people, and I am close to both of my step-parents, so I have a blended family that I am proud of. I have a lot of extended family and always rotated weekends and holidays between my mom and dad. I always wanted to be with my grandmother. My mom was always at work, so it came natural for my grandmother to be my household guardian. My grandmother was out of town the weekend I was molested so why I wasn't with my mother that weekend is still unclear to me because my other sisters were with my mom that weekend. My grandfather was a hard-working mechanic and excessive drinker. After the incident, I was removed from my grandmother's home and moved with mom. Living with my mom didn't work out because of our differences, so I was with my dad for a while. I didn't really process what happened to me until I spent hours at the hospital getting DNA and medical tests done. It was an emotional roller coaster from that point on. The key thing to know is that when I told someone about what happened to me it led to an investigation and that's when someone else who my grandfather molested spoke up as well. My god sister who used to live with us, who was much older, was a victim as well. This is why it is so important to tell somebody.

My pastor, church members, especially church members, family members, friends of the family turned the little information they received into "alternative facts" really quick. I heard the nastiest comments about a 12-year-old little girl ever in my life when I heard, "That's sad how she killed that man just because she wanted her own way." "Ugh, she's a hoe." "How could she do that to her grandmother?" "Her lil fast ass." Other than my parents and grandmother Viola; no one believed me. The perception that I was so spoiled to the extent that people thought I would go to the level as far as making false allegations against my grandfather if I didn't get my own way mentally stuck with me for a long time. When he died in jail while awaiting trial for the allegations I honestly went on a guilt trip. The last time I saw him was the evening it happened so I decided to attend the funeral and face what I thought would be my final goodbye. I wanted to see if he was really in the casket and dead.

I told somebody. I wasn't silent, but I was still ignored, ridiculed, and given the side-eye. People either tried to convince me that it didn't happen and I made the story up, or they just became silent to the conversation like I will one day forget. Well, it did happen.

It was a gloomy summer Sunday evening, and I was just getting out the shower after eating a good ole Carolina Sunday dinner. My grandfather was a great cook. I had the towel around me, and we passed each other in the hallway on my short distance to my room. The towel began to fall down on one side. I pulled one side of the towel up and held it close to me. I proceeded to my room and began drying off. I had my Beauty & the Beast pink and green nightgown laid on the bed to wear. It was my favorite. He knocked on the door that was cracked open slightly and notes at the usual "You gone clean my nails for me." "Yes," I replied. Even till this day, I am a gut type of person, and I did not have a good feeling about the energy in the house that evening. It was the usual "clean Granppie nails to earn money or snacks." Eat pork cracklins' and joke about how rough, dark, and dirty his nails were. We always kept finger nail clippers so we could clip and clean his nails. It became a childhood pastime of my sisters and me. I went in my grandparents' room and got in the bed to clean my grandfather's nails.

"I'm cleaning his nails, and he appears to be falling asleep or at least he had his bloodshot red eyes closed. I have one of his hands in mine. His other hand begins to massage my breasts. I leaned back expressing how uncomfortable I was. Then he slowly moves his hand up and down my thighs then up my dress. He gets on top of me, unzips his pants and pulls his penis out. He rubs his penis against and in my vagina. He does not penetrate."

The phone call saved me. The house phone rang, and he answered. To this day, I still don't know who it was that called. While he was on the phone, I found my way to ease into my room. He never came back in my room not even to see why I left. He didn't even check up on me. He fell asleep, and that's when I called my mom.

About seven years later, I was in community college and living back with my grandmother. I was driving east to Fort Lauderdale beach in tears and blood. Contemplating suicide, I thought I was going crazy. I wanted so much pain to end that I didn't know what else to do. I was the oldest in the house and the toughest, but I was tired. I didn't want anyone to know because if the guy I was dating didn't think much of me, then I couldn't think much of my own self to get help. My boyfriend at that time didn't understand how I could go from wanting to have sex with him to cold-turkey not even wanting him to kiss me on the cheek or show any affection. I went through these phases often. Out of his frustration, we got into an argument that led to a fight that led to me with a lot of bruises. And who would believe me, right? It would be my fault again, right? I faced my demons. I had a problem. I settled. I made excuses for people and myself. I was not healed. I was pretending. You know, just faking it and faking what I was going through. I was broken and tried to fix those wounds through my relationships with other men (that's another book) and being someone I wasn't (that's another book too).

All the things I was good at and passionate about as a young adult were gone. I didn't even know if dreams still existed. I cared less and less about college. I finally got to the beach, and I screamed. I cried and screamed. I glanced over to the passenger side on the floor and noticed an ink pen. I picked it up. I scrambled through all the junk in the back seat of my car and found a notebook. I started to write. I begin writing… "I forgive you. Dear Charles, I forgive you." The words came that easy at the moment. I wrote and wrote and wrote. It had to be at least 6 pages. I found a Sprite soda can. I stuffed all those pages in that soda can and got out the car. I walked towards the beach shores crying. I sat near the shore. I prayed to God like I've never prayed before. I threw the soda can into the Atlantic Ocean, and that's where the healing process began.

Throughout the years, I've experienced insecurities, identity issues, anger problems, turning down good men, staying with bad men, and always being on the defense and outraged just to name a few challenges. My parents sent me to counseling following the molestation, and over time they had to stop wasting their money. Counseling did not help me individually or help us as a family. In 2014, I returned to counseling on my own, and that's when it happened. I became free. I became a woman. Accepting and loving myself completely. I was tired of bleeding and started leading. It wasn't until 2015 when I stepped into womanhood.

From my healing heart to yours, I want to share what helped me to move on. First, I got rid of denial. I acknowledged that I was hurting. Then, I got to a place where I truly forgave my grandfather. I entrusted and built a strong support system. One of the biggest setbacks is when people think they can get through it alone. You cannot. Lastly, I started walking in my truth.

The number one thing that helped me was confronting my encounter. I spent so many years saving him in my heart by making up excuses that I did not notice I was harboring in so much pain. I confronted him even when he died because even though he was deceased everything I felt was still alive. Once I let go and forgave him, I began to use creative expression to learn who I was. I got to know me. Once I got comfortable with being myself, I noticed how powerful I was. Healing is a marathon. You don't become whole overnight. It happened. This is my story. I told somebody. Even if you are a witness, tell somebody. If you have suspicions, please tell somebody.

It is a fact that I lose keys all the time and it is frustrating. Imagine being locked out of your home, car, safe, or office space? It is usually a setback, right? So, when it comes to matters of the heart all we need is to understand the key. Luke 6:43-46 describes your heart like roots. Whatever you root yourself in that is the fruit you will grow. If you are rooted in evil, you will bear evil fruit. If you are rooted in love, you will bear loving moments. If you are rooted in malice and hatred, you will bear evil intentions and spite. The only way you can change your heart is to understand what rules it. No matter what you are going through your hurt can only be healed through Christ.

There's always something that just clicks, it's an "aha!" moment when everything just makes sense now. It's what my co-authors and I experienced. It's called The Brilliant Awakening. When I found my key; I turned my pain into power. I challenge you to "The Brilliant Awakening"... use the key.

Shannon Nealy

Shannon Nealy is a writer, speaker, and activist currently serving as a 911 Supervisor. She loves to volunteer for the Wonderfully Made Homeless Home, Not on My Watch Women's Initiative, National Black Police Association, and other charities. Shannon is an avid learner who loves to travel and explore new places, people, and things. She is completing her Bachelor's Degree in Business Administration and Ethics at Mid-America Christian University. Shannon believes in the power of positivity and is delighted to be a servant of Christ. Follow Shannon's journey on social media by searching her name (Shannon Nealy), #ShanShineSpeaks or visit her website: www.ShanShineSpeaks.com

"My 911 Call"

"911 What is your emergency?" is the way I was trained to answer calls 10 years ago when I started as a 911 operator. 911 operators have been portrayed on TV for years, sometimes realistically, but mostly those roles stray from the actual process, rules, and responsibilities of my experience. People who don't do the job are often times fascinated by what goes on behind the scenes. Many times, when I tell someone I work at 911, they tend to ask "What is the most stressful call you have taken!?" I came up with a quick response because Lord knows they did not want to know the actual most stressful call I have taken.

We all fear the unknown and the call that always increased my heart rate and poured adrenaline into my body was a call that went like this:

"911 What is your emergency?"

And then, from the other end of the line, complete silence. No response. No panicked breathing and shouted address, no screams, no sounds of struggle over a phone, or gunshots, no drunken shouting, no child crying uncontrollably…nothing. On calls like this, my heart would drop in fear. An open line is one of the worst types of calls a 911 operator can take. It means someone is there but they are either choosing to not say anything or, worse, can't speak because they are so afraid or are being kept from talking by their circumstance or fear of another person.

I now understand why I was so affected by that call because I was the silent caller on the other line. I could relate to being hurt by someone but afraid to tell anyone your truth.

The most stressful 911 call I have ever taken was my own 911 call. That may sound a little unorthodox, so let me explain: I was that terrified victim on the other end of the line, desperately needing help, but unable to speak. My period of pained silence didn't last seconds or minutes, it took ten years before I could finally answer the question I had asked others hundreds of thousands of times; "What is your emergency?"

You see, I was the caller in fear on the other end of the line, afraid to verbalize to anyone, even myself, that I was the victim of a despicable crime. I was a teenaged victim of a sexual predator. I was drugged and taken, without my knowledge or permission, to an unknown location and raped. I was completely at the mercy of a monster with no conscience and no morals. Even though I knew I was a victim of a heinous crime, I was silent. I was too scared to say anything. My pride caused me to be ashamed. I was silent due to fear of rejection, fear for my safety, fear of the unknown. I had chosen a career in which I urged victims of crimes to stand up for themselves and press charges against their attackers, but I could not convince myself that I was worth of the same justice.

In order to grant myself the same rights I encouraged strangers to pursue, I had to first experience ten years of similar calls at 911, the grief of losing my mother, counseling, and the unconditional love of God and support of my church, family and close friends. It would take every single one of those years for me to find the strength to finally state my emergency to myself, my family, my friends, and authorities. It took all that time to speak out loud about the crime committed against me by the "suspect". I will refer to him only as the suspect instead of the rapist because, to this day, he has yet to be convicted of rape even though he has been arrested multiple times and accused by several victims of the same violent act dating back to 1999.

The District Attorney has declined to prosecute this predator. I'm still waiting for the answer to the question I have called and asked the DA's office with no response, why?" How does someone get accused of raping multiple women but never stand trial. Why is this Predator still free to prey! Nevertheless, I digress.

I was born into a large family. My mom was a widow with two children and met my father, a divorcee with two children and they had a bunch of kids together! I was a product of that love and am number ten of the Nealy bunch. We were sort of like the Brady bunch but several more kids and we were the black version. My father was a Pastor, Businessman, School teacher and Accountant. He was very handsome and smart. I have very few memories of him because he passed when I was three years old. I remember my Mom being the head of the family from that point forward. My mother was a beautiful and strong woman in every sense of the word. Things in the Nealy house were not perfect by any means, but my Mom truly did her best with what we had. She was a proud Christian woman who raised us in church and lived a life according to her interpretation of the Word. Passing on her unwavering faith in God was the greatest gift she gave me and my siblings.

Between my siblings, nieces, and nephews, our house was always full of children and we loved to play church, reenact whatever our favorite show was, make fun of each other, dance, and generally be as loud as we still are today when we get together. I offer my sincere apology to all the public places in which we have been asked to, "keep it down".

By my teen years I had been to a range of schools from the hoods of Oak Cliff in Dallas, Texas to the suburbs of Moore, Oklahoma. I definitely developed a tough skin because I was constantly the new kid and had to learn to adapt.

Let's fast forward for the sake of time to my early naive adulthood. I was working as a secretary for that man who had become my sister's husband and my father figure. I had no reason not to trust this man who had been in my life since I was a child. So, when he offered me a drink one night at a public event, I had no reason to be suspicious. After that, my memories became hazy and out of focus, like a nightmare that rips you awake, screaming and shaking. I can clearly recall parts of that night because they are seared into my brain.

I became incredibly drowsy and remember trying to walk to the restroom because I felt nauseous. The next conscious flash I had I was vomiting down the side of the suspect's car. Then I blacked out again. I woke up with this disgusting predator on top of me, raping me. I tried to fight, I tried to scream but I had no control over my body and had no power to get up or defend myself. Then, I lost consciousness again. I woke up on the floor of my own apartment, surrounded by my own vomit. My clothes were disheveled and I was alone. I had never felt more alone. Part of me died that day. I knew what had been done to me and I knew exactly who did it. The crazy part is I still had to be around the suspect because, not only was he my boss, he was also a member of my family. How could I ever confront him or tell my family what he did without hurting my sister and ripping my family apart? I knew what needed to be done, but I just didn't THINK I had the strength to do it on my own. I lied to myself thinking if I did not say anything, I could eventually forget it.

God only knows how I was able to hold all of that pain and betrayal in for so long without breaking and to only think the tragedy in my life was not over.

My mother had survived two bouts of cancer and the treatments had been devastating to her health. My once vibrant and strong Mom had been weakened by this illness. She went into remission for a few years, but in 2011, she was diagnosed with breast cancer for a third time. I had the honor and pleasure to be her caregiver.

I started grief counseling after my mother's death. A part of my counseling included a review of significant events in my life. I was supposed to create a timeline of my life with all the highs listed up top and the lows of my life listed on the bottom. I could not list the rape on my timeline and the pain from this betrayal surfaced.

In 2015, after learning about another victim in the family at the hands of the same suspect, I finally "made the call to 911". I told my family, including the suspect's wife, what happened. The suspect was confronted by family and began to threaten me. As a result of threats and harassment, I pursued and obtained a victim's protection order through the courts.

The suspect was investigated and old charges against him were brought up. Felony charges were filed against the suspect for other crimes he had been accused of committing. Unfortunately, we are still in court because he is appealing the Victim's Protective Order (VPO) the Judge granted to stop the suspect's harassment. I am just asking him to leave me alone and do not understand why he continues to harass me.

I would have never imagined pursuing my journey to freedom, accepting my truth, and fighting for my peace by making a police report would cause me to lose relationships with family members, put me in jeopardy of losing my job and cause me to be called horrible names by some of my so called loved ones.

The rejection hurt me deeply, but it was a part of the process. I am now grateful for the rejection because it reminded me of my strength to stand alone and to get in tune with my creator who never leaves me.

Though I have not received what many would consider true justice, I have been given a measure of justice, though, in other ways; I have regained my self-worth, strengthened my relationship with God and my church, established powerful bonds with the people in my life who have come to my aid in my time of need, and I have become an advocate for victims of domestic violence, emotional abuse, and sex crimes. One of my mentors explained to me that justice is just not received in the court room, justice is also overcoming.

I have learned that some good can come from even the most tragic circumstances. Being a victim of rape nearly destroyed me and my Mom's death, while devastating, cascaded into a series of events that gave me the strength to finally come forward and place the call for help I had taken so many times before. At last, when I was asked, "What is your emergency?" I was able to answer in a loud clear voice and I will never be silenced again.

Tanisha Scott

Tanisha Scott is an entrepreneur (Owner of Testimonial Ink), a jewelry consultant, speaker and author. She is also a wife, mother and grandmother who loves her family. Through encouragement and compassion, Tanisha advocates for females who have experienced struggles throughout their lives. She believes that by sharing her experiences, being transparent and truthful, it compels them to move forward into their greatness.

"From Darkness to Light"

Lights... Camera... Action! These three words that resound in my thoughts repeatedly. I am the director of my very own cast of pretend, denial, and regret. We've worked together for over 20 years learning how to co-star with each other to accomplish a cohesive network of pretend for the finished product of belief. An Emmy for best actress I am sure to win. When I am acting, I report daily on set spending hours upon hours with minimal breaks, lunch, or sleep remembering the script of my lies reel by reel. I am aiming for faultlessness yet exhausted with thoughts of regret. This is my mind as I combat the disease of anxiety and depression. How did I get here? Why can't I escape from the haunting of my choices made, and why do I care how others will perceive me?

A teenage mother, a cycle I desired to break in my family, yet I too became a statistic while longing and searching for love. I gave birth to my first child at the age of 17. I was unwed and unsure of how I'd get through my senior year to graduate and if my dreams of college would remain a reality. My boyfriend was a freshman in college when we became pregnant. Accepting his responsibility of fatherhood, he finished his first year of college then left school to make sure he was there for his son and me. After delivering our son, I was homeschooled until returning to school. I did graduate on time and walked with my entire class that year.

In preparation of furthering my education, I would attend college, but I had to leave my now 11-month-old son behind with my parents. This decision alone was heart-wrenching for me; however, I always focused on the possibilities receiving a degree and providing a better life for the two of us. College was an adjustment and required lots of focus. I wasn't much of a social butterfly; while friends were out socializing, I'd stay behind thinking and wondering if my son was ok? We didn't have cell phones and today's technology. I was missing all the important milestones of his growth; I missed his first steps and his first birthday. This produced an overload of guilt for leaving him behind. There were many nights with my roommates unaware that I'd cry myself to sleep missing my son. I finished my first semester of college it was time for fall break, and I had already decided I wouldn't return. My only goal was to get back to my son.

Upon returning home, my boyfriend and I decided we'd both get jobs and move from our parents' homes, and we did so. Having a new place and a new child, although he wasn't newly born, it was our first time not having the help of our parents. Parenthood and our own place brought on an entirely new meaning of responsibility. As my son was turning two years old, we had a few weeks until our second child arrived. At the age of 19, I gave birth to our second son. Once again, I was in the cycle of dreams deferred. I was now juggling a household, taking care of a two-year-old a newborn and attempting to build a healthy relationship. I was working at a retail store longing to go back to school; once again school would have to wait.

Upon returning to my retail job after maternity leave, I was told the store would be closing. This was very untimely considering we had just moved into a new place. I was now unemployed with two children and no education. I had to now depend on financial assistance from the government until I found work again. Upon receiving my first monthly welfare check, I remembered sitting in the middle of my living room floor crying uncontrollably because this amount was not conducive to anyone for a living: this was my first and last welfare stipend. After strategizing a plan, my boyfriend and I decided it's time for me to go back to school. He would work during the day, and I'd go to school at night while he cared for the kids. Things were looking up. I was enrolled to become a CNA.

I had enrolled for classes adjusting into my role as mother and student. I had completed my clinical, it was almost time for certification, and once again I was pregnant. My newest child had not turned a year old. Like a balloon that has been blown up to full capacity and then let go for immediate deflation, every ounce of determination for a better life left. For days, I'd stay in darkness not wanting to take part in anything. I wouldn't tend to my children most days. My boyfriend practically raised our second son alone. I no longer had the hope I once had before as a student, mother, or girlfriend. My boyfriend and I discussed the situation, and he was supportive of my decision to terminate the pregnancy, although I knew this went against all he had believed and he truly didn't want to. I was not mentally prepared to have a third child. The morning of the appointment it was time to leave, and he decided he would not be a part of the termination. I had to call a friend and asked if she'd take me and she did. This became the tipping point of a decision I thought I'd never recover from.

My relationship was teetering on ending; he couldn't even stand the sight of me at times. Instead of us talking about what we had experienced, we lived as if it never happened. I secretly and slowly, like a festering infection, fell into depression. The decision to take control of my situation truly left me grief stricken, labeling myself as a killer with thoughts of doing the same to myself. The depression consumed me. I didn't get my CNA certification. I'd have anxiety attacks regularly. Therefore, I was sent for counseling which not only addressed this issue but multiple issues that I had suppressed throughout my life.

While dealing with anxiety and depression, I still had to remember my character role and put on my mask and play the pretend role of happiness, being a good mother, girlfriend, daughter, and friend when others were around me. On the inside I was in a dark place, seeing myself as an executioner, counterfeit, and condemned for my selfish actions, motivated by wanting to do better for my family. My depression would cause me to hibernate inside the house in gloom, never opening windows or truly having a social life, if anyone attempted to get close, I'd disconnect. The less I encountered others, the less I'd have to make-believe. I had convinced myself I was being a "good" mother to the children I had as if that would relieve the damage, fault, and disgrace from the decision to abort my last child. This didn't work. Before our second son turned two, I gave birth to my fourth child, third son.

I believed this was God's grace giving me another chance to repair my life with what I had single-handedly destroyed. I use the word repair because I was shattered and broken from my actions; there were so many pieces that not only had to be found and assembled but places strategically into its proper place for the healing to begin and God to use me as he had planned.

Once I found the true meaning of God's grace, and if I'd ask Him, He'd forgive me. It was then the healing process began. Instead of caring about how others perceived, me I began to search for how God felt about me. Upon Him revealing his love for me, I no longer had to despise myself or the month of February. This was the month I was to give birth to my unborn child. I now have two grandchildren born in this month, one on the exact date of my unborn child's due date. That's God turning my despair into joy.

The man that I thought would leave me for my actions and conditions, he married me, and we've raised our three sons together who are all adults now. My current journey is one of openness about who I am and where I've come from because there are so many women and girls who have the same issues and are playing the roles of "actresses." Some of them believe they aren't going to recover from choices made. I want you to know you will and you shall. It doesn't matter whether Man will forgive you for your actions. It's God's forgiveness that really counts. I now know that it's ok to share your imperfections with this imperfect world to let others find healing through your life story. Now that's a role worth auditioning and winning an Emmy!

Gia Sullivan

Gia Sullivan is a speaker, author, and blogger who enjoys working with nonprofit organizations to bring awareness and advocacy to mental health issues. Gia is a wife and mother of a blended family of an army veteran, nine kids and three grandchildren. She has an undergraduate and a graduate degree and has completed a NAMI (National Alliance on Mental Illness) Family-to-Family program.

"A Refining Mind from Defining Moments"

I remember thinking. *This feels gross. I don't want to do this. Maybe if I pretend to be asleep, he'll stop.* For what seemed like hours but was probably just minutes he laid on top of me writhing and fondling me and saying dirty things until he was "done." I was five, and he was the son of my parents' friend. For the next seven years, he and his older brother AND sister enjoyed their sexual engagements with me when the opportunity was made available. Since they would often babysit my sister and me, the opportunity came often. No, I didn't tell my parents. I was certain they would hate me. I would be an embarrassment to them in our little town, and I didn't want to get anyone in trouble. But, these were just things I was told to keep me compliant. Besides, my home life was good, and I didn't want to disrupt that. There were no drugs or violence in our home. We had family game nights and rode bikes together. Home was good. But during my sixth-grade year, while I was still submitting to the only one of my predators still left, I began noticing changes within me. I began hating myself. One day my parents were arguing, and this triggered my very first "breakdown." I went into my room and began throwing things around- blankets, pillows, anything I touched. My parents ran into my room. My mom grabbed me and held me. But it seemed I was watching all this from outside my body. That same year we moved, and I never had to see my childhood abusers again.

But unfortunately, I was to face more torment just a few years later. I stayed the night with a friend, and as many 15-year-old girls do, we snuck away to hang out with some boys she knew from a neighboring town. They picked us up down the street in their pick-up, and we went to the driver's house. We drank cheap alcohol and listened to 80's music. My friend drank way too much way too fast and passed out, so three boys focused their attention on me. Two of them held me down, and the driver of the pick-up promptly removed my clothes and raped me. I just lie there through the pain and looked at my friend passed out on the floor. Again, it seemed I was watching this event from outside my body. The boy didn't have to cover my mouth. I wasn't going to scream. I wasn't supposed to be there. I had been drinking, and I was wearing a miniskirt and a tank top. Truth is I wanted them to find me attractive, but I didn't want this. When he was finished, I went to put my clothes back on and was so embarrassed by the blood left on his bed. I was no longer a virgin. I hung out with them a few more times after that. I didn't want them to believe it was rape. I supposed if I was still hanging around them, I wasn't a victim... just a slut. I became more promiscuous and seemed to fall into depression a lot, although I didn't know that's what it was. And I continued to have a peculiar obsession with the subject of suicide. During my sophomore year, I experienced another "breakdown" when I threw my books down in the parking lot, walked into the girls' bathroom, and started screaming at people. I do not remember what I said or why I said it. Again, I watched it from outside looking in.

When I was just two months shy of 17, I married my military boyfriend against my mother's wishes but with my dad's encouragement. He had walked in on us having sex and was concerned I would get pregnant out of wedlock, an unacceptable consequence. Soon I learned of a life I had only seen in movies. While living in Germany, I was shocked and humiliated the first time he was physically violent towards me. He pushed me into a parked car. It was loud and in front of our friends. I hurt my knee and had to spend the rest of the day with a slight limp. He would hit me often, and I would occasionally fight back. Sometimes I would walk by and hit him just because I hated looking at his stupid face. Before I moved back to the states, we stayed in separate bedrooms. He would sleep with the dresser in front of his door because he said he was afraid of me. Then, it made me laugh. Now it makes me sad knowing that I got to that point. When he returned from Germany, we moved to his hometown of Galveston, Texas. Nothing changed except the introduction of drug use. The physical, mental, and emotional abuse from both of us was as rampant as ever. After four years of an on and off marriage and all the abuse, I found myself back in Oklahoma. I was divorced at age 21 with a GED, nine college credits, and a new boyfriend.

We moved to New Mexico and eventually went our separate ways a year later. He returned to Los Angeles, and I remained in New Mexico where I continued college and began a job as a cocktail waitress in a gentlemen's club. Soon, I made the inevitable switch to a dancer. For several months, I made my living hovering my nearly naked body over men, and some women to whatever music the DJ felt would get the crowd going. There, I met my next nightmare. I quit dancing and moved in with him. The first time he hit me he made sure I understood that I could never leave. How could I make this mistake again? It was shortly after this that I was first diagnosed with clinical depression and general anxiety. For the next few years, I endured punching and stomping by a man who was twice my size. I was locked inside the house with bars on the windows. I couldn't watch certain TV shows because I might like the men I saw.

One night he had me pinned on the couch with a gun to my head. He usually kept it under the mattress on his side of the bed. I had held it many times when he was gone, balancing its weight in each hand, thinking how I might use it someday on him or myself. But now here I was with that thought likely coming to pass. I still remember how cold the muzzle felt against my left temple. I just sat there with no emotion thinking Go ahead. Create a masterpiece with my brain matter all over this wall. I'm done. I guess he was put off by the lack of emotion because he turned and left without saying a word. One July, I prayed every day that he would find someone else and leave me… and he did! But he kept calling my new job and harassing me. I finally told him I had already told everyone about him and to look at him first if anything were to happen to me. He called me once more at work to apologize and said he would never bother me again.

Over a year later, I was back in Oklahoma. I had no one now. It was just me, and I was just fine with that, but then entered Jason. He started taking care of me and not taking advantage of me from the beginning. We married and added three children to those he already had. With his support and encouragement, I earned a bachelor's and a master's degree. Not everything was picture perfect, though. My husband knew there was something wrong just a few months after we married. I told him I had been diagnosed with depression and anxiety. He tried to get me to counseling, but I refused. When we had been married about 11 years, my husband talked me into speaking to someone at a behavioral health center. The result was 10 days of inpatient hospitalization. By the time I was discharged, I had been tentatively diagnosed with bipolar disorder and PTSD. Although I was not happy about my stay in the hospital, it was a turning point in my life. The "craziness" I sometimes felt inside actually had a cause. It wasn't because I was crazy or bad. Now I was learning how to fight it, control it, or work with it. I began medication and individual and group therapy. But as much as I was doing to help myself to become healthy I knew I was skipping a step. I needed to help others like me. I started a blog site to bring attention and understanding to the everyday issues faced by those with mental health concerns. I advocate for positive changes in mental health programs and connect with nonprofit organizations that encourage and support those with mental health conditions.

Chasity Travis

Chasity Travis was born on December 8,1985 in Sayre, Oklahoma. She is a mother of three and loves growing her spiritual relationship with God. After obtaining her bachelor's degree, she immediately completed two master degree programs, one in Adult Education-Training and the other in Human Relations with LPC. She is the founder of the non-profit called Educating & Empowering the Mind & Body, Inc. As the CEO of her own behavioral health counseling agency, Recovery Achievements LLC, she is blessed to focus on her passion by helping those in need. As a Licensed Professional Counselor candidate, Chasity is approved to treat mental, behavioral, and emotional disorders through providing therapeutic services.

"Repositioned and Focused - Philippians 3:12"

As I reflect on how adults avoid or refuse to focus on the prominence of sexual and mental health regarding our youth, I can better understand the lack of educated information that I was not taught at an "immature age." Today, I have answers, feelings, and knowledge that would've been of great benefit mentally and emotionally during my younger years. I was taught the basics to living life as a child, such as getting up for school, riding the bus to church, playing outside, good hygiene, and cleaning. A very important necessity to our youth is education on sexual health, functional and positive relationships. Learning how to handle emotions, especially in the aspect of the opposite sex, could create healthy relationships and boundaries. Growing up, this was a taboo topic in my house, like many other households. I am a prime example of how the lack of sexual and mental education can impact a young girl in today's society.

In my younger days, I was always book smart, eating my grandmother's wonderful cooking and being the best at making my mother's coffee with sugar and cream. My father was an alcoholic and drug user, who stayed in Arkansas most of the time. He didn't show us what to look for in a boyfriend or man, how could he? As far as my siblings, I looked up to my oldest sisters who were in college, while the boys dropped out in junior high and learned to bond with the streets rather than family. When our mother was on the phone with our older siblings and having coffee conversations with our grandmother, my little sister and I would hear about college trials and tribulations as well as jail, gang, and police encounters. One specific situation that had a great impact on our family was when my brother was sentenced to 35 years in prison as an accessory to murder. At 12 years old, I didn't fully understand the mental capacity of heartache and pain, but I knew my emotions were on a roller coaster from being angry at and sad for him at the same time. Other days, I came home and literally watched my other brother steal televisions, my gold jewelry, and many other things out of our own house just to sell or pawn for money and drugs.

My ninth-grade year, I met this boy who lived on my street. He would kick me, spit on me, and shove me for no apparent reason. I had been taught by social media, school, and few family members, "It is normal for boys to flirt and court by teasing, hitting, and being obnoxious." Eventually, I felt that he liked me, even though I was embarrassed by the way he bothered me. Then, I had enough courage to beat the crap out of him, I was fed up, at least that is what I thought. After accepting and allowing his way of flirting and courting, he introduced me to something new. It was sex, a taboo topic that I was unknowledgeable and inexperienced with. It was only one time that I gave in, and that was all it took. A dark room full of denial, depression, and shame had my name written all over it. With no prenatal care for seven months because of me keeping this stressful and depressing pregnancy a secret, and the abortion clinic explaining that I was too far along, I became a mother at the age of 15. I was "A baby having a baby." I kept a secret that was so powerful it divided me from others and affected my development at a crucial time for self-growth and identity. How could this have happened to me? Was it the lack of education and talks about sex or the introduction of inappropriate touch from my immediate family member a few years back? I was all over the place, far from what a 15-year-old should have to endure.

My faith in God, my son, and the goals for my educational success kept me on track. I managed the many obstacles of being a teen mom and moved forward. I continued to master the educational path as I always have and obtained my bachelor's degree. It was the relationship with men I could not grasp. Relationships are difficult, especially when you lack an example of what a positive and mature one truly consists of. Six years later, I met a guy who was about four and a half years older and seemed to be very gentle and loving; at least that is what I thought. He claimed to work with his grandfather in his carpentry business. To keep it real, I was still sensitive and vulnerable, although in my mind I was strong and confident. It didn't take long before I found out about the other side. You know, the drug dealing, physical and emotional abuse, and mean fighting streak that not only occurred with me but also everyone else. I was such a loving person, and I felt sorry for people who played the victim, causing me to trust easily, my downfall. The jealous and controlling ways were plain as day, even to others, but why was it overlooked and not obvious enough to me? One night I woke up confused. I went to the mirror, and I had a black eye and snatched out hair from my head. I don't even remember this happening because it happened in my sleep. Literally, I was knocked out. He laid there accusing me of his made-up accusations, as he always did. I went to the hospital, and a police report was made. I still loved him, I thought, but he wouldn't allow me to move on. I tried. Kicked in doors, busted out windows, door handles ripped off, lab tops and flat screens cracked. This guy would destroy everything and then bring flowers, money, and diamonds to make it up.

My family was disgusted with him, I hated him, and I started to hate myself. Love makes you do stupid things, especially when you don't know "real love." I became pregnant. Depressed and mentally drained by this drama infested person and ways. Pregnancy is already draining to a woman's body and soul, but to have a person be disrespectful, destructive, and mentally and physically abusive was devilish. During this time, I was attending college for my first master's degree, which helped me to escape. After the birth of my baby girl, I was able to think clearer and realize that things were about to change for the better. I prayed for help in escaping this nightmare of what many people call a relationship. My mother and little sister began to talk about killing him before he killed me, while my brothers said they are only a call away. If I didn't answer the phone, a feeling of discomfort and unease would fill my family's heart. I knew that it was getting real and something had to give before the trigger was pulled. I could not allow any more hurt to myself and family. Prayer warriors were in full effect, and my goal was to relieve myself and my family from this toxic, mentally draining situation. My baby girl was only five months and my son eight years old when he was sentenced to five years in prison. I wish jail not on a soul, but I was the happiest woman on God's earth when I heard the news. I survived and could peacefully progress without manipulative distractions.

Today, my past experiences are the obstacles I overcame. My heart is forgiving, and I love and forgive all. Grudges, I hold none. Now that I have completed my second Master's Degree in Human Relations and obtained my Licensed Professional Counselors candidacy, I have learned many theories and answers to why people choose to react in the way they do. Many individuals do not have interpersonal social skills, causing issues in appropriate relationships, communication, behaviors, etc. Many of our parents lack these skills and have no interest in instilling them within their children, maybe because they don't know how or where to start. It is important that our children learn how emotions affect learning, behaviors, and relationships. Social development is a critical necessity to the success and stability within one's life. Information and support can help the challenges associated with sex and mental well-being. Educating and empowering ourselves and our youth will help aid in the understanding of what love, respect, healthy relationships, and social development should be. Grateful am I for the many seasons I have endured and conquered. I am proud to say that I am not perfect, but the fight for resilience through each situation forced me to stay strong and overcome the adversity. As parents, we are the initial advocates and teachers for our children. It is our duty to educate and empower our youth with mental and sexual education at an appropriate age.

Mishondy Wright-Brown

Mishondy Wright-Brown is a Director of Nursing and a wellness and community advocate and educator. Because minority communities have higher incidences of certain illnesses, Ms. Wright-Brown is passionate about changing the view of wellness in order to encourage minority communities to take charge of their physical, and mental, wellness. She lives in the DC Metro area and promotes living a lifestyle of wellness wherever she goes. She is currently planning her wellness groups and programs. Mishondy is the Founder of "Don't Touch Me!"™, an organization to end molestation through awareness, education, and empowerment and the author of, "No More Secrets: How to Discuss Molestation With Your Children" and "The Black Girl's Guide to Wellness: A 21-day Guide to a Healthier, Happier You!"

"Becoming the Woman I Needed"

I was a newlywed. I was beginning my life with a man with whom I thought that I would build my empire. We had just moved into our own place and were looking forward to "christening" the place. I had taken my shower and was prepared to make love to my new husband and I could not. Almost instantly, I lost the mood. He was confused as to how I could change so quickly. It did not stop him, though. He continued to his goal.

Since it had only happened once, I did not pay much attention to it. Unfortunately, it did not stop there. When I bathed before bed, I could not perform with my husband. I. Just. Could. Not. He tried all types of things to "get me in the mood," but his efforts were futile. I wanted to go to sleep and maybe try again in the morning. Over the next few weeks, however, it began to bother me. I could not understand what was happening. As my husband became increasingly angry, it caused me to go on a quest to figure out the root cause of this issue.

"Was it Dial soap that our molesters used when they made us bathe one another?" I asked my brother. I was desperate for answers.

"Yes," he replied. "Remember? That is the soap they used on us over and over again." Memories came rushing to me. My once-perplexed brain was filled with images that caused me to cringe. I thanked my little brother for that information, and I hung up the phone. Then, I cried.

I was between five and six years old – the oldest of three children. My brother was a year younger than I was, and we had a younger brother who was a toddler. My mother worked a 3:00 pm to 11:00 pm shift at one of the local rubber plant in our town. My father was not in the home, so my mother solicited the assistance of a babysitter to care for us while she worked. I remember the woman very well. She was a tall, Christian woman who lived in the projects up the street from my grandmother's house – where we were living, at one point. She was a sweet woman. She loved the Lord, and she made me feel safe. She had two children – the eldest, a son and the younger, a daughter. I don't remember exactly how old they were, but they were older. I recall that the male had a jacket that I now know to be a letterman's jacket. It had a gold letter on it, probably from one of our local high schools. The female looked to be middle school-aged. Everything seemed okay, except one-day-a-week. The woman attended church services, at night, weekly. Since my mother picked us up after 11:00 pm, the woman would ensure that we had a bath. Once-a-week, her children were responsible for ensuring that it was done.

For some reason, the children had my brother and me to bathe together. I guess using the same bath water was convenient. The brother and sister would sit in the bathroom, together, as my brother and I took our bath. They instructed us on how to bathe, which was innocent enough until the instructions were for us to bathe one another. My brother was told to "wash her chest" as the teenagers watched. Voyeurism. My brother did as he was instructed to do. I did not know that it was wrong; I just felt "funny" as it was happening. Then, I was told to "wash him down there." Because I did not know that it was wrong, I did as I was instructed. I remember my brother having a "weird" look on his face. The teenagers, however, looked to be smiling. Was I doing a good job? Would that make them like me now?

I asked that question to myself because those teenagers had been mean to my brothers and me. They would give me a stick/switch/belt and demand that I hit my toddler brother. If I did not hit him hard, they would chant, "harder, harder." My baby brother suffered abuse at my hands. Once he cried hysterically, they allowed me to stop. When they walked away, I would comfort my baby brother. Other times, the teenagers would bully us in front of their friends. I remember them "scolding me out" in a circle. Big kids looked on as I was called "gap-toothed, black, ugly, and bald-headed" just to name a few. Those insults hurt me so badly that I was willing to do whatever it took to make it stop, including bathing my brother "down there."

More memories surfaced. After the baths, I was instructed to go into the bedroom, on the left, with the boy as my brother went into the bedroom of the girl, on the right. I recall having to put my mouth on his private part. When I resisted, I was threatened with the iron that sat on the ironing board against the wall to my right. Because I did not want to be burned, I did what was requested of me. Over and over, week after week my brother could not quite articulate exactly what happened when he went into the room – at least not that I can recall. What I do remember is that he was traumatized. Just like me. Bath time was a time for shenanigans. My innocence was snatched from me. My view of love and relationships formed from a deep, dark place which I spent years trying to understand. There was so much pain; it was so painful that I repressed it. I pretended like it never happened. Until the Dial soap...

That experience led to other less-than-desirable experiences. It became easier for predators to spot me in a crowd: damaged, broken, hurting, and vulnerable. I made some decisions based on those experiences. I did not know who I was. I operated in brokenness. I walked in doubt, rejection, and feelings of unworthiness. That broken little girl became a broken woman who chose to have a child as a way of experiencing love. At 18 years old, I became a mother.

I had no idea that motherhood would be the catalyst to me becoming whole. It is not what you may be thinking, however. It was not a fairytale experience and the sight of her face that changed me. Quite the contrary, becoming a mother seemed to shine the light on the "issues" that I had. I was never loved (well, I never felt loved), so I had no idea how to love someone. To me, love looked like sexual acts and missing parents. Love looked like not having an advocate as men ripped and pulled and tugged at me. Love looked like pleasing others in order to get the madness to stop. It was the molestation of my three children by their father, my husband, at the time, for me to "woman up" and find, and give real love.

Yes, he molested them – his children – and I did not have a clue: maybe because I was still broken, maybe because I was trying to hold myself together, maybe because I did not love myself enough to love my children in a way that would have put me in better touch with them. The answer was found in self-love.

My story of transformation is far more convoluted than I am expressing here, but here is the gist of it: Because I did not love myself, I was incapable of doing anything healthy. In trying to make sure that my little people were doing well after their molestation, I found myself. My initial focus was to ensure that these people recovered from their molestation. I put myself on the back burner and focused on their healing. Once they were better, I realized that the molestation caused so many issues with my children – and with me. I spent my life in survival mode, not realizing that I was not truly "living." In trying to make life better for my children, I discovered that there were many people who were just going through life without the tools necessary for them to lead a full, healthy life. In that, I found my calling. My desire was to stand in the gap for others to learn how to love themselves through any adversity that they found themselves in – like I learned.

The day that I learned to love myself was a perfect one. I was on a journey to becoming a better version of myself, but I had no idea when my dream would come to fruition. One day, as I was brushing my teeth, I looked at myself in the mirror and started talking to myself: "I am so proud of you!" I did not stop there: "You are an amazing mother of three wonderful children. You are doing a great job. I am so proud of you! I love you!" As I said the words, "I love you," tears rolled down my cheeks. I repeated that phrase over and over again. I looked at myself and realized that, for the first time in my life, I loved the woman looking back at me. That day, I became the woman I needed. The woman I'd become spoke to the little five-year-old girl within me and I became whole. I was awakened!

Helpful Resources

SEXUAL ASSAULT

NATIONWIDE: National Sexual Assault Hotline (800) 656-4673
Oklahoma Coalition Against Domestic Violence & Sexual Assault State Office
www.ocadvsa.org
24 Hour Sexual Assault Hotline: (405) 943-7273
Rape Hotline (405) 943-7273

DOMESTIC VIOLENCE

NATIONWIDE: 1-800-799-7233 | 1-800-787-3224 (TTY)
24 Hour Domestic Violence Hotline: (405) 917-9922
Oklahoma Safeline: (800) 522-7233 | *You can ask about getting a (Victims Protective order) on this hotline*
Heartline: 2-1-1 or (405) 848-CARE
VPO (Victims Protective Order)

> Protective orders are available to people who have been physically abused, stalked or threatened with imminent physical harm by a family or household member. For more information on protective orders, getting a protective order, what types of protective orders there are, how long do they last, steps for getting a final protective order and what happens afterwards, visit the following website:
> http://www.okdhs.org/purpleribbon/howto

(Legal Resources) http://oklaw.org/resource/domestic-violence-resources-and-links

MENTAL HEALTH

NATIONWIDE: SAMHSA's National Helpline 1-800-662-HELP (4357)
Suicide Hotlines: (800) 273-TALK (8255) OR (800) SUICIDE (784-2433)
NAMI Oklahoma Helpline: 1-800-583-1264

This book is a collaborative effort with:

NOT ON MY WATCH WOMEN'S INITIATIVE |
WWW.NOTMYWATCH.ORG

The mission of the Not on My Watch Women's Initiative is to provide a gateway of advocacy, awareness, support and resources for women and girls affected by domestic violence, sexual abuse & assault and mental illness.

Made in the USA
Las Vegas, NV
16 June 2023

73105374R00057